The Heart Handbook

your guide to getting back to the basics of love...

Also by

Laura Mangin McDonald, MA LPC

―――

Christian Insight for Life…
For Every Day
(2013)

Perspectiva Christa Para A Vida
…Para Todos Os Dias
(Portuguese Edition 2013)

How You Think…
Determines The Course Of Your Life
(2014)

The Heart Handbook

your guide to getting back to the basics of love...

Laura Mangin McDonald, MA LPC

CHRISTIAN INSIGHT FOR LIFE

Requests for information and comments should be addressed to:

Christian Insight for Life, P.O. Box 452796,
Garland, TX 75043-2796

ISBN-13 978-1983482557
ISBN-10 1983482552

Cover Design: Megan Hurd and Kori Sparks
Author Photo: Brandon Hurd
          bhurdphotography.com

Printed in the United States of America

www.christianinsightforlife.com

*"Above all else, guard your heart,
for everything you do flows from it."*

Proverbs 4:23

ABOUT THE AUTHOR

With compassion, humor, Spirit-led insight, a well-used Bible and a whiteboard, Laura offers a straightforward and accessible application of the Word of God to understanding patterns of relating and relationship skills, setting healthy personal boundaries, overcoming fear, and healing emotional heart wounds.

Over the years, Laura heard from her clients a common theme of pain and isolation experienced in relationships, which gave her insight into developing an engaging and relatable approach to uncovering and healing the deep-rooted and unexplored emotional trauma we hold in our hearts that keeps us in bondage, preventing us from forming and enjoying intimate personal relationships with God and His people, as God intended.

Laura is a Licensed Professional Counselor with over 30 years experience in individual, marital, family and group counseling, including inpatient hospital settings.

Laura also speaks, writes, and facilitates training seminars for organizations on team dynamics, crisis intervention and conflict resolution. Laura and her husband, Rod, are the founders of Christian Insight for Life, a Garland, Texas-based teaching and discipleship ministry. Laura is the author of several books, including the popular devotionals *Christian Insight for Life...for every day* and *How You Think...Determines the Course of Your Life*.

ACKNOWLEDGEMENTS

This handbook is dedicated to all my courageous clients over the past 30 years. Thank you for trusting me with your hearts and stories...they are woven into the pages of this handbook with my love and prayers.❤LMM

CONTENTS

Chapter Two

Chapter Three

Chapter Four

Our physical heartbeat gives us life, but our emotional heartbeat determines how we live the life we're given. Proverbs 4:23 sums up this truth: *Above all else, guard your heart, for everything you do flows from it.*

Most who are reading this handbook would probably describe themselves as a Christian and feel they are in a close relationship with Jesus. Many who are reading have known Jesus since they were a child, but don't feel very close to Him or His people. Others who are reading have been in church most of their life and they know a lot of Scripture, but they question if Jesus is the only way to Heaven. And then there's a whole lot of people who are reading this handbook who aren't sure what they believe. We have many differences as a group of people– different experiences that have shaped our different beliefs. But there is one need that we all have that is the same and that none of us can live without–this need is woven into the emotional fibers of every human heart...

We. All. Need. Love.

God placed the same set of emotional needs inside of every human heart so that we can experience the love we need in relationship with Him and others. But because we are imperfect humans living in an imperfect world...our needs for love are often not met in relationships during our growing up years like they should be. This results in us experiencing unmet emotional needs that morph into emotional and psychological issues. But we are not left without help; God promises that He will heal our heart with His love. And that's my purpose in writing *The Heart Handbook*. It's your guide to getting back to the basics of love. This handbook is the culmination of 32 years of my clinical experience that will explain why our emotional issues manifest and how we are to heal them God's way, in a practical and applicable easy-to-follow format that's concise and straightforward.

Here's the layout: I've condensed the standard emotional growth and development tables into four progressive emotional stages for a quick reference guide. These four emotional stages are divided into the following four chapters:

• internalizing love
• identifying boundaries
• integrating our heart
• implementing the truth

Each chapter begins with an overview that gives a brief description of the developmental stage it correlates to, the basic emotional needs for that stage, and the emotional deficits that manifest into symptoms if emotional needs are not met. Within each chapter are 10 different examples that I see in my practice that are divided into three parts: situation, symptoms, and solution.

On the next page is the heart "Snowman" diagram that I developed and use in my practice to illustrate how the promises of God renew our mind, heal our heart, and seal our spirit. You can also access my brief teaching videos on my Christian Insight For Life Facebook page using this model. ❤LMM

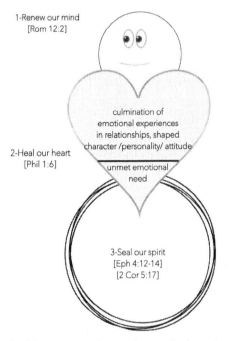

1-Renew our mind
[Rom 12:2]

culmination of
emotional experiences
in relationships, shaped
character /personality/ attitude

2-Heal our heart
[Phil 1:6]

unmet emotional
need

3-Seal our spirit
[Eph 4:12-14]
[2 Cor 5:17]

To heal the unmet needs in our heart as God promises, we have
to bring all of our mind, all of our heart, and all of our spirit
into relationship with Him and then with His people
to receive the grace He gives that binds
up and heals our unmet needs.

Chapter One

Internalizing love –
the non-negotiable needs

*"Then Christ will make his home in your hearts as
you trust in him. Your roots will grow down into
God's love and keep you strong."*

Ephesians 3:17 (NLT)

Our first stage of development is internalizing love…the non-negotiable for bonding and connecting in relationships. God placed these needs inside every human heart; we need: bonding, safety, nurturing, trusting, being loved, and having someone to love. When we consistently experience these emotional needs being met during our formative years, we develop a deep sense of belonging in our heart.

Over the years I've met with hundreds of people who love God and profess that God loves them, but they don't feel like they belong. They pray, memorize Scripture, are actively involved in community groups, Bible studies, and serving in church leadership, but they can't shake the sense that they don't belong. It's like they are on the outside looking in; they don't feel like they are connected or a part of the people who they've been doing life with for years. No matter how much more they increase doing and giving, these actions don't negate the constant sense of not belonging that they feel. The things they do matter, and they need to be doing them, but it's what they are not doing that is perpetuating their feelings of not belonging.

The answer to belonging is opening up our heart and bringing all of it into relationship with God and His people to give us the grace we need to heal emotional needs that we didn't get while growing up.

God wired every human heart to be loved. Most people profess a need to be loved–they know that love feels good, but they aren't able to articulate what love looks like...they just know that they want to feel loved. Wanting to feel loved is a God-given desire. So for us to understand and experience love the way God designed it, we have to know the basic emotional needs that He wired inside of every human heart. We need to feel safe, nurtured, desired, accepted, validated, encouraged, and known in our innermost parts in our significant relationships.

When we consistently experience these emotional needs being met, they culminate into us feeling a deep sense of belonging and we know that we are loved. Our knowing is experiential–we know we belong because we have experienced belonging in relationships and this sense of belonging translates into being loved! And this belonging roots and grounds us in God's love! No matter where we go or what we do we have an emotional home in our heart that's experienced belonging and being loved. Understanding this connection enables a person to unravel the contradiction of believing they are loved, but feeling like they don't belong.

Being raised in a home where our emotional needs are met during our first stage of development enables us to experience the sense of belonging and feeling loved even when we're apart from our loved ones. However, no perfect home exists because we are imperfect people living in a messed up world—inevitably our development will be negatively impacted by natural disasters, deaths, diseases. But the worst injuries come from the people who are suppose to protect us and don't—these kind of injuries run deep. If we've experienced parents and caretakers who inconsistently attached, were emotionally unstable or unavailable, came in and out of our lives, inflicted emotional, physical, sexual, and or spiritual abuse...then we will have emotional deficits. *These emotional deficits don't go away when we grow up—* they manifest into negative symptoms, dysfunctional behavior patterns, and psychological issues. Some of the more common ones are distorted thinking, shallow relationships, excessive caretaking, addictions, depression, feelings of guilt, a sense of unreality, irrational fears, anxiety, agitation, rage, lack of purpose, and inability to bond and attach in relationships.

We would have no hope if we were left with the reality this life dealt us, but thank you, Jesus, we do not have to stay stuck...God has made a way! The following 10 situations are examples of how our unmet needs manifest when they go untreated, the symptoms most people experience, and the three-part practical application solution rooted in God's truth to get us on the road to recovery. I pray your mind, heart, and spirit open up to the revelation of grace, truth, and love that the Holy Spirit wants to impart to you in this chapter. ❤LMM

1.Where time and trauma collided….

*"He heals the brokenhearted
and binds up their wounds."*

Psalm 147:3 (NIV)

Significant relationships during our formative years shape and influence every aspect of our emotional development. These relationships determine how we perceive ourselves, others, God, and the world in general. It's God's design for us to literally internalize how to love and learn from our family, friends, teachers, coaches, church leaders, and others who have the authority to influence our lives. Our experiences in these relationships are recorded and written on our heart as points of reference to give us the help we need. But the sad reality is the same people who are supposed to help us, are also…

The. Same. People. Who. Hurt. Us.

The hurt we experience in these relationships is where time and trauma collided in our emotional development. Until we begin to have some insight into the significance of these injuries, we will go through life with an *emotional limp*. God promises to heal our broken hearts and bind up our wounds, but we have to actively connect to the structure His grace encompasses. I use a whiteboard to graph clients' emotional timelines to identify where time and trauma collided and the negative patterns of behavior that developed. To say this visual illustration of a person's life on the whiteboard is validating is an understatement. Quite often during these sessions there are long moments of silence where the client and I will stare at each other and then back at the board because we witnessed the the Holy Spirit transforming information into revelation right before our eyes! This is God's desire; He will give us insight into our past to understand how it is impacting our present, and the wisdom to know how to move forward to be restored and healed. When we get to a place where we can identify our patterns…we have opened the door to solutions! *Our patterns do not lie*…they are truth-tellers that backtrack our steps of development and point us to the places where our unmet emotional needs where injured and where time and trauma collided!

To heal the unmet needs in our heart as God promises, we have to bring all of our *mind*, all of our *heart*, and all of our *spirit* into relationship with Him and then with His people to receive the grace He gives that binds up and heals our broken heart. These three steps explain our responsibility in receiving the grace God gives.

1- God's Word renews our mind. We are to memorize, confess, and profess God's Word over our life to renew our mind. We are to take every thought captive that doesn't line up with God's truth. But what many people do not know is…the thoughts that they are taking captive are directly hardwired to the emotional trauma that they experienced in their heart. For example, a person could diligently professes 1 Peter 5:7: "Cast all your cares on Him because He cares for you", for years to line up their anxious thoughts with God's truth and not feel much improvement in their anxiety. But their lack of improvement isn't because God's Word isn't true or that God doesn't care for them. What they do not realize is, their lack of improvement is due to their unmet emotional needs not being healed in their heart. This unmet need will continue to drive the anxiety as a cry for help until it's healed. And until a person understands this truth, they will continue to try and convince themselves of a healing that they have not experienced. I'll explain in the next truth, number two. (Rom 12:2; 2 Cor 10:5; Ps 26:2-3)

2- God's Word heals our heart. It is full of power and promises to heal the emotional injuries in our heart. We cast down the the strongholds in our mind that come against God's Word. Then we go to our heart and trace how the stronghold is hardwired to our emotional injures so that it can be stopped! But we can't heal these injures independent of actively being connected to all the elements that Gods' grace provides. In the case of the person with anxiety, they will continue to hit a wall in healing until they ask God to search their heart and rely on His unlimited grace and wisdom for help. Many continue to seek Christ, but they do not reach out for the next step of God's created order: the healing God facilitates through his body of Christ.

That's us! God Himself is present in the Body of Christ (Eph 4:16). His Spirit lives is each one of us (Eph 2:21). We seem to get this when it comes to laying our hands on each other for healing (James 5:14-16), but often we pass on this precious promise when it comes to opening up our hearts and letting the Body of Christ heal our injured and damaged emotions (2 Cor 6:12-13). We are to love God and each other (Mt 22:37-40). This is a topic I spend a lot of time on processing with clients because it seems to be one of the best kept secrets in God's church. I pray you will not pass on the healing that our Father will facilitate through us, the Body of Christ, to receive grace, help, healing, direction, discipline, connection and to be held together with Him! (Col 2:19; 1 Ptr 4:10; 1Cor 4:7; Eph 4:15-16; Mt 18:20)

3- God's Word seals our spirit. We are a new creation in Christ—nothing can change this truth! But for God's promise to bring this truth to fruition…we have to participate in the process listed in numbers one and two, above. The person who's working through their anxiety understands the promise in 1 Peter 5:7: "Cast all your cares on Him because He cares for you". This person is connected to God and casting their cares by relying on His wisdom to search their heart to what's driving their anxiety either through direct revelation from Him or through the Body of Christ. For complete healing, their relationship with Christ and His Body involves their entire being: all of their head, all of their heart, and all of their spirit. The three work in tandem and with God and His Body to heal the tender part of the anxious person's heart that went into hiding long ago.

As the anxious person brings all of their unmet emotional needs for safety and nurture back into relationship, sits across from another person who has the Spirt of God's love flowing through them, and gives this person the tenderness and warmth that they didn't get years before, then the rest of 1 Peter 5:7: "because He cares for you", comes to fruition in this person's heart. They no longer have to try and convince themselves of a healing that they have not experienced…because they are experiencing the healing God promises in relationship with His Body of Christ! The part of the heart that was hidden was invited, accepted, and loved, which made it safe for their real self to be restored in relationship. This restoration put an end to the lack of safety and nurture that drove the symptoms of anxiety. Now, someone needs to say, "Amen"! God's design is amazing, we just have to choose to participate in the process. (2 Cor 5:17; Eph 2:10, 5:13-14)

My prayer is this insight will give you a better understanding into how to incorporate all the elements of healing as God designed us to. ❤LMM

2. Don't ever believe the lie that it's too late…

*"I sought the Lord, and he answered me; he
delivered me from all my fears.
Those who look to him are radiant; their faces are
never covered with shame."*

Psalm 34:4-5 (NIV)

Many believe the lie that it's too late for their life to turn around due to the situations they're currently in or have experienced in the past…but it's never too late for God to help us! A situation can consume, overwhelm, and paralyze you for a period of time, *but never for a lifetime*! I've sat across from people in my office for over 30 years and listened to their situations: molestations, murders, affairs, divorces, abortions, suicides, addictions, disabilities, stolen virginities, prison time, family secrets, eating disorders, financial crisis, sexual perversions, chronic illnesses, learning disabilities, DUIs, pornography, obesity, anxiety, depression, distortions, rejection, perfection, despair, hopelessness, and the list goes on.

If I were a therapist who didn't believe in the redeeming power of Jesus' love, I wouldn't have a word to say to this kind of pain when I'm sitting across from people who seek counseling. I'm licensed to practice, give diagnoses, facilitate therapy, etc…but my credentials and experience do not have the power to offer hope in hopeless situations—I need the backing of a Savior Who holds together all we see and don't see while promising us hope in the middle of it. With His backing, I can promise every person I counsel that there's hope in their hopeless situation *because it's His promise.*

None of us ever have it completely together—we will always have some kind of faith challenge because we need a Savior every second of our life. But if you grew up in a family where your negative behavior was minimized or love was withheld when you disobeyed, you will have a hard time believing our Savior won't pull away when you disobey. Some families teach it's weak to ask for help— no matter the severity of the situation, but especially if you brought it on yourself by some kind of careless behavior. If so, you've probably developed a false sense of humility and resist or refuse help for fear of being seen as weak and irresponsible. Maybe your family didn't know how to give warmth, empathy, and understanding when you were hurting…so you learned to cut off those needs in your heart. If you did, you probably don't know what you're feeling, what you need, or how to open up your heart and ask God and others to be with you when you're hurting.

Wherever you are today and whatever you've been through, I can promise you because it's God's promise—it's never too late for Him to help you! Your part is to turn to Him: "those who look to Him are radiant; their faces are never covered with shame!" (Psalm 34:5). Here are three steps that will help you open up your heart to God so that He can help you in your situation:

1- Many people have not experienced the bad parts of their heart being exposed and loved— so they hide when they mess up. This is the worst thing they can do because…*they turn away from the love they need to turn around*! A statement many clients make is: "I don't want to be a hypocrite", meaning they don't feel like they can pray if they've been away from God or are in the middle of sin. My response is: "pray, baby, pray"! When we need help calling out to God is our lifeline! The power and love of Christ can take on any situation we're in. He's not intimidated, shocked, or overwhelmed, but we will never know this truth in our individual situations until we take the risk to call out to Him. (Rom 8:1, 37-39; Col 1:17; Heb 11:1)

2- God hardwired our heart to need help from Him and His people–this built-in need keeps us humble and keeps us connected. When we embrace our humility and need for connectedness, we have our needs met and we mature along the way. It's how we "attain the whole measure of Christ". Asking in general always puts us in a vulnerable position, but if we were taught it's a weakness to ask...we will resist and refuse the very help that we need to turn around from the situation we're in. (Eph 4:13; Prov 3:34)

3- Our emotional needs for warmth, empathy, and understanding are put in our heart by God– these needs have to be met in our heart in healthy relationships for us to face, and move through, hurt in life. Not all families know how to give these things because they learned their patterns from previous generations who didn't know how to give them. *Learned patterns perpetuate from one generation to the next until they are interrupted and replaced with new, healthy patterns*. If you're reading this, you are taking the first step to interrupt the learned pattern of behavior that has kept you closed off from getting the warmth, empathy, and understanding you need in life. Your willingness to open up your heart to God's help from Him and His people, promises to begin the process of healing in you and give you hope...no matter what kind of situation you're going through. (2 Cor 1:3, 7:2; Phil 1:6)

A situation can consume, overwhelm and paralyze you for a period of time, *but never for a lifetime.* I pray you won't ever believe the lie that it's too late for God to help you. God started a good work in you and He will bring it to completion until the day you see Jesus face-to-face. God's love redeems and restores what was taken, given away, or never received...will you let God's love comfort and help you today? ❤LMM

3. Stop– in the name of love…

"For everyone who asks, receives.
Everyone who seeks, finds.
And to everyone who knocks,
the door will be opened."

Matthew 7:8 (NLT)

Over the years in my practice I've listened to Christians quote Matthew 7:8 hundreds of times. Often it's in reference to desiring to feel loved, cared about, and provided for. These three desires are part of the core needs that God places in every human heart. Since we can't meet our own needs, we have to ask, seek, and knock on God's door. Jesus tells us to be persistent in doing these things and that God will provide. But what I've come to realize is that most people don't believe this to be true for their lives based on their personal experiences.

People tell me that they have asked and not received, sought and not found, and knocked but the door wasn't opened. Some people have banged, beat, and kicked the door down out of frustration, hurt, and anger. Others have walked away believing God is mad or punishing them for an unforgivable behavior. And a bunch just push down their disappointment and sadness; then they vacillate between trying to win God's approval and being bitter about the needs He's providing to others. But here's the worst: most won't admit their negative emotions, or when they do, they don't take ownership. Until they do, they can ask, seek, and knock their entire life and never fully receive, find, or see the the door open because of their unwillingness to work on their issues...*God's way.*

And their unwillingness perpetuates their distorted thoughts that manifest into negative relating skills to the people who God sends to help them. It's an insidious cycle that neither ends nor satisfies and keeps them stuck! All of us have needs because God put them in our heart. Also, all of us have needs that weren't met because we live in a messed-up world with imperfect parents. And all of us have to admit our negative emotions and take ownership of them, if we want to receive, find, and go through the open door that God promises.

God works through our present relationships to provide our emotional needs that weren't met in our past relationships. *Our unmet needs happened in the context of a relationship and they have to be met in the context of a relationship.* This is where the road forks and we decide if we're going to stop in the name of love and do things God's way or lean on our understanding and do things our way. If we decide to stop in the name of love, here are three concepts rooted in God's truth to get us started:

1- Guard our heart. We are responsible for guarding our heart above all else—it determines everything we do. But we have to guard the way God instructs us...not in our understanding. When we do, He will make the justice of our cause shine like the noonday sun (see Psalm 37:6). Now somebody needs to say, "Amen and thank you, Jesus"! God's way lets good love in with the risk of being hurt, but also with the promise of being healed. Good love is God's model for love and it always trumps bad love, which is man-made and dependent on human traditions influenced by spiritual powers in this world. We are not exempt from bad love harming us, but it can never overtake or own us...because it has to stop in the name of love...God's good love that continues to do a work in us until we see Jesus face to face! (Prov 3:5, 4:23; Col 2:8; Ps 37:5-6)

2- Bring all of our heart into relationship. All of our heart has to be present for all of our heart to be healed. Any part of our heart that we hold back can't be healed. Many people are stuck in old hurt that is in their heart because they didn't have some, most, or any of their basic needs met. They reason that they've brought all their heart before God, but He does not meet their needs. But what's happens is they box God in, and it's usually related to a verse like Philippians 4:19: "My God will meet all your needs". And God does–He's our only Source, but He has a gazillion resources that He works through. We have to be willing to open up our heart and trust His provision of resources. One of His resources is us, the Body of Christ. God will give us what we didn't get. He promises to "place the lonely in families" and "He heals the brokenhearted", but we've got to bring all of our heart in relationship and open up to the love He sends! (Phil 4:7: Ps 68:6, 147:3)

3- Take ownership of patterns that resist and reject love. In the first paragraph we talked about the needs of being loved, cared about, and provided for not being met for many of the people I've worked with over the years. In any area in which our emotional needs weren't met, we will develop an *emotional deficit*. These emotional deficits drive behaviors that result in negative relational skills. For example, a person who desperately wants to connect will resist and reject the very love she needs by defensively guarding her heart and not be responsive to genuine gestures of love from others. Another example is that this person will be verbally abrasive to those who reach out to her. Both of these negative relational skills keep people from getting too close. It's so sad, but I see people do this all the time—it's impossible to heal and connect apart from being loved in healthy relationships. (2 Cor 6:9, 6:12, 7:2, 7:6; Job 42:11)

We couldn't do anything about our unmet needs as children, but as adults we don't have to stay stuck in what we learned back then. We have a say now, but we have to—stop...in the name of love! Will you? I pray you will, so that you can live the life you were purposed for! ❤LMM

4. A false source…leads to a false solution

"Don't let anyone capture you with empty philosophies and high-sounding nonsense that come from human thinking and spiritual forces of this world, other than from Christ."

Colossians 2:8 (NLT)

We live in an age where we are bombarded with the latest discovery of "finding our true self". I've listened to a lot of people over the years sit across from me in my office and tell me their story of the time and money they spent searching to find themselves. The sad ending with a search of this kind is it always ends the same: the true self wasn't found, but disappointment was. The search for our real self happens when we walk on the path God made for us long ago. This isn't my promise, it's God's promise.

The truth is…just because a person refers to love, grace, and faith—doesn't mean they are speaking God's truth. Be on guard to who you're listening to, endorsing, and following on social media. Many are deceived by their own delusions of grandeur; they claim their way leads to discovering the true self that's inside every person and when we know "who we are", we can live a fulfilled life. Their statement is true, but their way is wrong; there is only one way to know our true self and His name is Jesus! The rationale used for finding ourself is illogical— think about what's being said. If a person doesn't know who they are, then how are they going to know when they find themselves??? They propose to have found the key to unlocking the secret to living an abundant life...but Jesus already gave us the answer over 2,000 years ago!!!

Here are three unchanging truths to embrace to develop into the authentic, real you:

1- There's no trauma, unique situation, or unusual dilemma in our life that's beyond the parameters of God's redeeming love. But every time we ponder possibilities outside of God's parameters– we step off the path He's made for us and we give the enemy more rope to hang us with. (1 Ptr 1:13; Ps 119:18; Isa 32:3)

2- If God is for us, who or what can come against us? But if a person seeks a false source...they will get a false solution! God designed our mind to be logical; we are to be informed, gain knowledge, and seek answers to solve problems, but we must be led by His spiritual discernment. God's truth remains unchanged, despite the changing eras, popular opinion, and ideas of mankind. We're not left to the uncertainty life imposes; we can be certain of the provision and power of Who lives in us. (Rom 8:31; Ps 102:27; Isa 42;16)

3- Finally, we do not have to grope through life and hope we can find our "true self"; we have a Father Who divinely designed us to be our "true self". God chose and loved us first, knows our name, calls us His masterpiece, gave us a unique fingerprint, DNA, and purposed everything about us to make a difference in this world. But we forfeit the fulfilled life He promises and subject our mind to mental torment when we reduce His wisdom to our level of human understanding. (1 Cor 2:5; 2 Cor 2:10, 11:13-15; Isa 32:4).

Who are you listening to, endorsing, and following to find the real you? ❤LMM

5. We have to get real– if we want to heal...

"Confess your sins to each other and pray for each other so that you may be healed. The earnest prayer of a righteous person has great power and produces wonderful results."

James 5:16 (NLT)

Don't pass on the power of confession—it's integral to our intimate connection with God and His people, our character development, and emotional healing. Many of the people I work with come to their first session with a negative impression of confession because of their experiences of being shamed, estranged, and condemned. I get sad and mad when I hear about these kinds of situations because hearts were unnecessarily wounded and God's heart was completely misrepresented. Plus, the things that were said could be nothing further from God's truth! Confession is agreeing with reality: God's truth and our heart issues related to our sins, struggles, and need for help. Confession is our means to get real so that we can heal.

Any part of our heart that has unconfessed sin or struggles will separate us from the love of God. A separated heart is an isolated heart and an isolated heart eventually takes on a life of its own. And when it does, it's where *crazy* happens...affairs, abuse, addictions, and debilitating patterns of behavior wage war and take over in the heart. I believe Proverbs 4:23 is clear in what we need to do: "Guard your heart above all else, for it determines the course of your life."

Here are three ways we can guard our heart and stay on the course God calls us to by actively participating in the confessional process:

1- Confession cleanses us. Confess everything... not just the big things. Nothing is too insignificant or unimportant nor is anything too far gone to be confessed. God's love is big enough to handle anything we need to say– we can't shock Him, we won't stump Him, and He won't pull His love away from us...ever! As soon as we begin confessing, He begins cleansing and transforming our heart. He will give us wisdom without finding fault. (Acts 3:19; Eph 5:14; James 1:5)

2- Confession gives clarity. God's truth is a mirror showing us where we are in our sin and struggles and where we need to be to walk in the freedom we're promised. When we normalize and accept the reality that as long as we're breathing we will have some kind of sin or struggle, we have positioned ourself to quickly take ownership. Doing this daily with God and on a regular basis with a trusted inner circle of people who we can rely on to speak truth in love...will keep us on a path of authentic character growth while fulfilling the purpose God put in our heart long ago! (James 1:23-24; John 8:31-32; Eph 2:10, 4:25)

3- Confession heals us. Confession has to take place with people who are rooted in God's truth and grace....it's the only way to reconcile, transform, and heal the deep wounds of the heart. This kind of disclosure is beyond vulnerable, but the power of God's healing grace that's experienced is undeniable! When I'm facilitating a person in this kind of confession, it's on holy ground because the

Holy Spirit is guiding the process. I'm using my clinical counseling skills, but I'm submitting to the lead of the Holy Spirit while witnessing the power of God's grace doing an emotional heart surgery in the person I'm helping. I have no words to adequately describe this holy exchange other than to say it's an undeniable, tender, warm, and powerful presence of God's love that is physically felt, understood, and received by me and the person whose eyes I'm looking into. When we can purge all the unconfessed issues in our heart and look back into the eyes of those around us and see their loving and kind eyes accept and love us...*we are healing and we know without a doubt that we are a child of God*! (James 5:16; Prov 28:13)

If we want to heal...we've got to get real. Getting real is some of hardest work we will ever do, but it leads us to the best place we need to be—developing and walking in the freedom we're promised! Getting real is about bringing the hidden parts of our heart into relationship and getting the love, acceptance, and grace we need to turn around. I pray you will embrace the gift of confession so that you won't stay stuck one more day. ❤LMM

6. Good friends are like good tread on our tires...

"Two are better than one, because they have a good return for their labor: if either of them falls down, one can help the other up. But pity anyone who falls and has no one to help them up."

Ecclesiastes 4:9-10 (NIV)

I see it in my practice, statistics prove it, I personally have had my life changed by it, but most of all it's God's design— it is good friends! Good friends are like good tread on our tires: they give us the traction we need to stay on course...they encourage, celebrate wins, stand with us, give grace, speak truth, heal our hearts, and console us during the losses of life. I am so grateful for my good friends!

Connection is our most basic need in life—God put this need in our heart. Good friends are one of the ways God sends us the answers to meet our connection needs. But many people have developed distorted views of God's design for friendships due to the hurts they've experienced in their past relationships. They believe they don't need people or that finding good friends isn't for everyone. Although their views are valid based on the hurt they've encountered—what they believe about not needing people or having good friends couldn't be further from the truth!

The only way for us to heal from the hurt that we've experienced in relationships is for us to go back into into a healthy relationship and experience being healed. Hurt happened in the context of a relationship and hurt has to be healed in the context of a relationship. There's no other way to do it because it's how God designed it! Most refuse to do this for fear of being hurt again, but all their refusal does is forfeit any future friendships.

But if a person is willing to heal God's way and open up to finding good friends...He will help. It's His design. Here are three steps to consider when thinking about good friends:

1- Good friends aren't a *luxury*...they are a *lifeline*! Connection is our most primary need— this is God's design. He is relational and He created us in His image as relational people. He designed us to rely on Him and His people, the Body of Christ. This is summed up in Romans: "In Christ, we though many, form one body". (Rom 12:5; 1 John 4:16)

2- God's love promises to heal the hurts we experienced during our formative years. For example, If we didn't get the warmth, nurturing, and encouragement we needed during our emotional development we can experience these needs being met in our friendships. *God will facilitate this process we just have to be open to it*. (Prov 27:9; Ps 68:6)

3- God created the Body of Christ, His church— that's us! We are to be in meaningful relationships with each other so that we can comfort, help, hold, encourage, and heal one another with God's love flowing through us: "but God, who encourages those who are discouraged, encouraged us by the arrival of Titus", and we are to "mourn with those who mourn". (2 Cor 7:6; Rom 12:15)

I pray you will embrace godly friendships. Who are you hanging out with? We need to be asking ourselves this question because who we're hanging out with will determine our ability to heal and stay on course! ❤LMM

7. Getting the love you need…

"You have let go of the commands of God and are holding on to traditions."

Mark 7:8 (NIV)

We are made to connect deeply and intimately in relationships– to be understood, known, and heard. These experiences culminate with us being loved and knowing how to love in return. This is God's design–our heart is wired to instinctively search for love outside ourselves so that we will connect with God and His people. As we connect, we internalize love into our heart so that it takes root. The love we take in from others becomes our love–we are able to love ourselves, others, and God, *it's our love transplant.* For this to happen we need healthy people, relationships, and experiences. Some people were raised in stable families and others in chaotic ones, but no person was raised in a perfect one. And none of us have reached perfection in our relational skills– there's always room for growth. I am specifically making the point because I've come across some Christians in counseling who believe they are teetering on the edge of perfection, but it "ain't so". All of us need ongoing grace, truth, and direction to know how to get the love we need and relate to each other as God instructs us to.

Most people I counsel genuinely desire to follow God's ways for getting the love they need in relating to others as He instructs. They intellectually understand the concepts, but they keep getting stuck in the practical application. The problem isn't in their *effort*–the problem is in their *patterns*…the way they learned how to relate. For us to follow and carry out God's ways, we need practice in learning His ways in healthy relationships while unlearning our old patterns of relating. Our mind agrees with God's ways because we desire to get out of our relationship ruts, but our heart kicks and screams because it defaults to the predictable patterns it knows...even if they are unhealthy! Crazy, isn't it???

Anyway, authentic change is hard work because our old patterns have deep roots in our heart– they have been our reference point for relating to people our entire life. We need lots of experience in healthy relationships to learn the patterns of relating God's way, which means we have to be vulnerable to get the love we need to move forward. If you have a history of unhealthy relationship patterns, you will need to learn healthy ways of relating in "safe hands" with a Christian licensed counselor, counseling pastor, Bible-based process group, group therapy, Christian retreat, or in a paraprofessional Christian-based group that meets on a regular basis.

Here are the three non-negotiable characteristics that have to be present in a relationship for you to experience getting and giving the love you need with God's ways, while learning healthy patterns of relating:

1- Full ownership and disclosure: taking full responsibility for the behaviors that have manifested in your heart and sharing them with God and His people so that all of your heart can be accepted and loved by God and His people. This kind of disclosure is the *bridge of vulnerability* we have to walk across to experience God's grace being manifested through His people. (Eph 3:17; 1 Ptr 4:10; Heb 10:24; Mk 7:13)

2- Emotional presence: there is power in presence —knowing a person is for us enables us to move through life's inevitable trials. We take their love in our heart and it takes root. It's like a "love transplant"; it becomes our love, to love God, ourselves, and others. This is God's design for us, being rooted and grounded in His love so that we have enough love in our hearts to love Him and others while carrying out the purpose He put in us, and having hope while doing it! (Mt 5:2, 22:37-40; Eph 3:17; Heb 6:19)

3- Accepting grace: this step is the most difficult part of the process because our heart is so raw and exposed. If you've never experienced being unconditionally loved in your worst times, you will be flooded with emotions...all the years of denying, holding back, minimizing, trying to prove you were good enough, and pushing back tears. Humbly accepting God's grace from His people and letting them love you is the first pattern of behavior that all the other new patterns of behavior must rest on. (Rom 8:1, 8:31, 8:37; Eph 3:16-20, 4:25; James 5:20; Gal 6:1)

You do not have to settle—you can get the love you need, but you will have to be vulnerable and open up your heart in relationships while unlearning the negative patterns of relating that are ingrained in your personality. Will you commit to seeking God and being involved in these experiences with His people so that you can? ❤LMM

8. Of course you're anxious and agitated...

"Cast all your anxiety on him
because he cares for you."

1 Peter 4:7 (NIV)

Anxiety and agitation are at the top of the list for reasons people seek counseling and coaching. Most people who set up an appointment report that their current situations are the reason they're experiencing anxiety and agitation and they want to know how to stop feeling the way they do. I agree that their current situations can *trigger* these feelings, but I explain that it's the pattern that was ingrained in their heart as a child that *drives* how they respond to their situations. Many doubt my explanation at first. The typical response is: "My situations are stressful and what does my childhood back then, have to do with now?"

Here's how it ties together. Anxiety is an internal alarm that reminds us we can't control our external environment–this reality sets off feelings of agitation because we feel stuck and without choices. When we're children, we need grown ups to soothe and validate our fears–to help us to structure our thoughts in response to this big world. If a child didn't get this, they are going to feel alone and overwhelmed, which manifests into anxious and agitated feelings. If the manifestation of anxiety and agitation continue, they ingrain into the child's personality structure. Many describe these feelings as an ever-present uneasiness– a silent voice that warns them: "be on guard". And. It. Is. Exhausting!

God designed our mind to be logical and reason probability, but we're to do so with the spiritual discernment of the Holy Spirit and from the encouragement of those who love us. Attempts made apart from this model result in us being anxious and agitated. We can catapult our thoughts into the future for weeks, months, and even years when we entertain probable outcomes regarding our life. What's crazy about this thinking is that we didn't go anywhere and none of the negative scenarios came to pass, but in our mind, it's as if we lived out each disastrous one!!!

If you can relate, you are not alone. Let me explain what happens:

1- Our thoughts are hardwired to the core beliefs in our heart. Our core beliefs determine how we see ourself, others, and the world in general. Our core beliefs are formed in the context of our significant relationships during our formative years. If our significant relationships were not reliable or emotionally available to us, we will default to self-reliant behavior because we could not rely on the adults who were supposed to be handling situations, so we had to learn to cope the best we could. This resulted in us not learning how to ask for help. And the behavior of self-reliance became our ingrained pattern and it's how we related to the world—it's what we know. (Mk 7:8)

2- Even though you may desire to rely on God's Word...you don't know how to because you still default to the ingrained patterns you learned long ago. You're doing what you were taught and you can't do differently until you have new experiences to replace your former ones. Your emotional experience is your only point of reference and it will trump your desire to rely on God's sufficiency. (Rev 3:17)

3- For you to increase your trust and learn how to rely on God when you're anxious and agitated, you need new emotional experiences with accepting, trustworthy, and warm godly people in safe settings like licensed Christian counseling that is individual or group process, pastoral counseling, seminars that are biblically based and led by licensed professionals, and the like. These are safe settings where you can practice opening up your heart to help, while having people guide you. Being vulnerable and opening up your heart to internalize the care of people who are for you will not be easy, but you're not alone anymore...you have God's help and His people to help you. These experiences replace your original self-reliant experiences that kept others from helping you. And your new emotional experiences with God's people bridge your trust and reliance on Him! (1 Thess 3:12; 1 Ptr 2:2)

Amazing, isn't it? But this is God's design– whatever we missed during our early development, we can still get after we've grown up! We do not have to stay stuck because we missed out on something early in life! Will you seek the experiences you need in order to learn how to rely on God and His people instead of yourself? Are you ready? ❤LMM

9. Time passes…hurts don't

"But I will restore you to health and heal your wounds…"

Jeremiah 30:17 (NIV)

Unresolved hurt distorts how we see…it obscures our view of living in the present because life is experienced through unresolved issues from the past. Hurt disguises itself in our relationships as blame, anger, agitation, disappointment, suspicion, and a need to prove one's worth. Old hurt morphs into psychological issues like anxiety, depression, and phobias—it also seeks to be healed in substances, addictions, compulsions, performance, statuses, being busy, and people pleasing, etc. Hurt doesn't go away when ignored, it shows up as a vague emptiness, an unidentified uneasiness, or a general sense of feeling wrong on the inside. Hurt keeps on hurting…until it's heard and healed.

Over the years in listening to people talk about their hurt, I've observed two opposing sides that people often get stuck in: either they don't make the connection of how their their hurt manifests as mentioned in the above examples, or they are very aware of their hurt and wear it as a badge of their identity. Sadly, both of these views enable the enemy to steal, kill, and destroy the life Jesus promises us. But the good news is there is no hurt that's too unique or so unusual that it escapes the scope of Jesus' redeeming and transforming love that He promises us! For us to participate in the promise, we have to open up our heart to the healing process with God and His people.

Here is the practical application of the steps that enable us to participate in the supernatural promise of healing:

1- Our healing process begins with grieving–seeking and submitting to the guidance of the Holy Spirit, asking Him to search our heart and show us where we've been hurt. Don't be alarmed by the flood of emotions– it's the culmination of years of denying hurt, holding back tears, and minimizing feelings, while trying to overcome the deep-rooted shame that something was wrong with you. Grief is God's gift to us–*it's the only pain we willfully enter into,* but God promises the pain will lead to healing and hope. Grief acknowledges what was lost, stolen, given away, or never received. Grief validates our experiences and says what happened to us matters, even though it was years ago! Grief is good pain– it activates the healing process and lets the love of Jesus soothe, comfort, and give hope to every part of our broken heart. Until His love floods us, we're a prisoner in our own pain. (Ps 139:24-25; 2 Cor 3:17; John 10:10)

2- Hurt *happened* in a relationship and hurt has to be *healed* in a relationship. We have to reach out and open up our heart to godly people who are equipped and balanced in God's grace and truth. This is unnerving because it places us in a vulnerable position–most have been avoiding vulnerability up to this point in an attempt to protect their heart. So what many do is rationalize pushing forward and healing in private with God. God can certainly heal us with one touch of His hand, but His healing doesn't negate our need to connect and process our pain with His people. We are made to grieve in relationships–*it's how we feel and experience* God's love incarnationally, while processing and gaining insight into how the hurt interrupted our emotional development and growth, and manifested into psychological and emotional issues in our relationships. We also need the Body of Christ to experience the fullness of God's grace. The bottom line is...hurt happened in a relationship and hurt has to be healed in a relationship—it's God's design. (2 Cor 3:18, 4:8, 6:12)

3- Staying in relationships—it's the hardest! Something I explain to people all the time is even after we have major revelation and internal heart transformation where we're making visible progress...we still have to be cognizant of our former negative behavior patterns. This is just common sense: our old patterns are deeply ingrained and our new ones aren't yet. For example, if your old pattern was to isolate when you were ashamed, embarrassed, mad, sad, etc... don't panic and think you're backsliding, but do be prudent and be ready to push back on your old patterns that might try to derail you. If you do relapse into it— don't beat yourself up. Instead, reach out to someone and share what happened. Many clients tell me: "I realized what I was doing so I didn't need to reach out to anybody". But this defeats staying in relationship! I'm not saying to call your friend at three in the morning when you realize it, but in the next week or so when you're having lunch and you're being real, tell your friend about your experience. People who care about us, care about the things we care about. The only solution to our hurt is love...the love God gives directly to us and the love He dispense through His people. (1 Cor 3:9; 1 Ptr 4:10; 1 Thes 5:11; Isa 61:1-3)

This is what the real Christian life looks like...*being saved doesn't exempt us from being hurt.* Hurt is part of life– it can't be avoided, but it doesn't have the power to steal the victory we're promised, unless we try to heal our hurt apart from God and His people! God is waiting and His people will help. Time passes...hurts don't. Will you open your heart so your hurt can be healed? ❤LMM

10. We do differently– when we believe…differently

"Then you will know the truth,
and the truth will set you free."

John 8:32 (NIV)

Have you ever been told these things:

• if we really wanted to change– we would
• we just need to try harder
• we need a better plan

We heard these; we gave it our all, and we failed miserably. Let me save you some time and energy- embrace this truth: we will do differently…

When. We. Believe. Differently.

To believe differently requires three components: grace, truth, and time. These three components must be dealt with in our hearts where our issues developed. Many try a lifetime to change outward behavior that can only be healed in the inner parts of the heart.

No matter what we've been through we do not have to settle for just getting by or having to be on guard to protect an injured part of our hearts. We will be hurt in this life, but we are promised that we will overcome. Here's what we have to do:

1- Desire opens the door, but grace enables us to walk through it. We can't produce grace—it's a gift from God. God gives us grace directly from Him or dispenses it through His people. Grace fuels us with the love and courage we need to look at the parts of our hearts that we've locked away and the parts that we certainly don't want others to see! It's this very exposure that shines the light of God's love on the issues of our heart and begins to break up the strongholds that keep us in hiding. *What we bring in the light…loses its power*! The more we internalize God's love, the more we're able to deal with our hearts' issues that hold us back in life. (Rom 5:1; John 5:4-5, 17:21)

2- We need God's truth to move through and on from our heart issues. This requires a deep work of the Holy Spirit. He has to show us and empower us with the ability to overcome the hurt that has held us back; it's His job– He's our Comforter, Advocate, and Voice of Truth. He does the internal work in our spirit, and then we need our godly support system to externally hold us accountable. God's grace never runs out, and only with His truth will we move on from the hurt in our hearts. His truth hurts– we don't like it, and many times we find it unfair…we can ponder, debate, and speculate until we take our last breath, but His ways work! We choose to follow Him–He will give us the strength to do so. (Rom 9:1; John 8:31-32; Phil 4:13)

3- We don't want to take the time that time requires; only in God's timing will we overcome! Thank you, Jesus, we are overcomers because the Overcomer lives in us…we're not left to the mercy of the bad things that happened to us, the poor choices we made, and/or strongholds that threaten our livelihoods. (Ecc 8:6; 1 Cor 10:13; Heb 10:23)

We have a Redeemer, and He will redeem every part of our lives that we release to Him! Are you ready to believe differently so that you can do differently? ❤LMM

NOTES

Chapter Two

Identifying boundaries–
knowing where we begin and end

"Guard your heart above all else,
for it determines the course of your life."

Proverbs 4:23 (NLT)

Our second stage of emotional development is identifying boundaries–knowing where we begin and end. Boundaries serve two major functions in our life:

1- They define us by distinguishing our individual identity and our ownership for everything inside of us, which is a culmination of our personality structure, behaviors, attitudes, beliefs, desires, feelings, opinions, choices, abilities, and thoughts.

2- They protect us by letting good things in, keeping bad things out, and kicking out the bad from our formative years when we didn't have a say. If someone crosses our boundary lines in a negative way, it's our responsibility to escort them off of our property. Protecting also exercises our right to say "yes and no" and listen to the the internal alarms God prewired inside of us to know when our body is fatigued, lonely, or senses some kind of danger.

God wired us to instinctively pull away and develop our individual identity, while staying deeply connected in relationships. Although this is a natural and needed process of our growth and development designed by God, it's also the area where many of our problems are found because we're confused about where our boundaries begin and end. Here are two illustrations that explain the difference between healthy and unhealthy boundaries:

1- Imagine two complete circles that are pliable and decide to come together to closely connect. Being pliable allows them to push up against each other while still maintaining the boundary lines that separate them. They enjoy the connection while respecting the distinction of individual lines; this allows them to experience different feelings, desires, and ideas without getting lost in the other circle. This is an example of healthy boundaries: two people who willfully connect and enjoy each other, but maintain their separateness by being responsible for everything inside their individual circle.

2- But when two circles come together and cross over into each other's boundary lines because they were not taught how to maintain separateness while being close, taught to have a false sense of responsibility for what's going on inside the other circle, or taught to cross the circle lines if they want something the other circle has…the result is disastrous! Fights about who's responsible for what and comments like: "you made me", "I didn't have a choice", "it's your fault", and on and on. Although this is a simplified example, it represents the chaotic life of people without boundaries.

Boundary development begins around age two and is ongoing our entire life, but it's during our formative years when some of our most important development happens. This is the time when the foundation of our character is being constructed and internalized into the core of our identity in our heart. *And this is why we can't talk ourselves into having healthy boundaries...* boundaries are understood conceptually in our head, but they are executed emotionally from our heart. People who try to execute boundaries without personal insight into why they struggle with them to begin with will be eaten alive with guilt, frustration, and a false sense of responsibility.

When we understand healthy boundaries the way God designed them, we can love deeply without losing ourselves. But if we experienced people violating our boundaries by imposing guilt messages, pulling their love away, controlling our feelings, abusing us, or not helping us with safe limits...then we are going to struggle with carrying through with healthy boundaries in our life. These struggles lead to a host of emotional and psychological issues.

Before you begin to read the following symptoms, ask the Holy Spirit to guard your mind and heart while giving you wisdom. This list is meant to help you, not overwhelm you. But don't be naive, the enemy is prowling around and he wants you to believe that it's hopeless for you to change. Remember the enemy is a liar! Here are the most common emotional and psychological issues that develop when a person has boundary injuries: blaming, enabling, depressed mood, difficulty being alone, disorganization and lack of direction, feelings of being let down, false sense of responsibility and obligation, anxiety, impulsiveness, inability to say "no", isolation, masochism, guilt, panic, passive-aggressive behavior, procrastination and inability to follow through, resentment, borderline and histrionic personality disorders, substance abuse, eating disorders, thought problems, obsessive-compulsive problems, victim mentality, and inability to stand up to conflict. Be careful to not beat yourself up if you're struggling being consistent in setting boundaries. Many people think it's just a matter of learning boundaries and then implementing them, but this is not true.

The following 10 situations are the boundary issues that I most see in my practice that people are prone to get stuck in, how the unmet needs manifest when they go untreated, the symptoms that most people experience, and the three-part practical application that's rooted in God's truth to getting on the road to recovery.

I pray you will receive the clarity and confident expectation of the Holy Spirit as He instructs your spirit to face what's driving your unhealthy patterns of relating, gain insight, and make the necessary changes to have healthy boundaries in your life.
❤LMM

1. Knowing who to trust…is so hard to do!

"Don't waste what is holy on people who are unholy. Don't throw your pearls to pigs! They will trample the pearls, then turn and attack you."

Matthew 7:6 (NLT)

We don't have to live too many years before we experience the harsh reality of being exploited, betrayed, or taken advantage of in some way. No person is exempt–it's part of living in this messed up world. Our best effort at being wise is undermined and we're left laying flat on our back… but we don't have to stay there! God promises that we can overcome the wrongs done to us and gain the insight we need to be more prudent, but it requires us to constantly put our faith in Him and line up our beliefs with His. And that's where our real problems begin because…you, me, and everybody else like to lean on our understanding instead of on the One Who saved us. It sounds ridiculous to even write this, but until we bring that reality in the light, we can't deal with it. But because we have a good Father, each time we turn to His grace and truth, His power is perfected in our weakness–thank you, Jesus!

After we get back on course and gain insight and understanding, we have to find a balance between not being paranoid, but still being prudent in our observation of a person's behavior, right? And that's why knowing who to trust is so hard to do! But we're not left to grope in the dark and hope to find trustworthy people to open up our holy things to– God's Word gives us direction and discernment. We just have to be taught how to use it.

Here are three truths that will help us to discern another person's character:

1- Pump up the "discernment muscle". We have to be taught how to discern trusting others. To get a good assessment of a person's character, we need to watch their behavior in different seasons. The best predictor of *future* behaviors...is a history of *past* behaviors. A lot of people have a hard time doing this with a person who's making positive strides. The hard reality to swallow in this is that positive strides are great progress, but until they become ingrained patterns, they are not reliable predictors of behaviors.

As soon as a stressful situation hits, we default to our ingrained patterns. This is great when we have healthy coping skills, but disastrous when we have unhealthy ones. I see this all the time with people who are "delivered" from drugs and alcohol. There is no doubt that God's hand delivered them from their addiction, but the person wasn't delivered from the character issues that were being covered up by the drinking or drugging. They have to go through a season of consistent counseling to address and resolve their old character patterns and learn new ones. This is where I ask my client to stop and unpack all the information and experiences to date— understanding the reasoning behind their decisions and if they are taking full responsibility for their decisions. I do this to help reinforce that there is no rush or doubt. We need people who are for us, to stand with us, and who help us "look at" our thoughts. This helps reinforce healthy thought patterns and dismantle unhealthy ones that we may have allowed to weigh in on our decision making. Also, when we know others are for us...we have a safe place to turn to when we face conflict. It's God's design for us to experience the incarnational love of Jesus. (Prov 1:3, 1:5, 11:14, 13:20)

2- Take the time you need to make healthy decisions. I remind clients to exercise their right to not be rushed into a relationship—and if in doubt...

Take. More. Time.

There's no rush. In fact, if you find yourself getting caught in some loop of rushing, let that be a red flag. If you're not in a completely comfortable place in the relationship, then do not move forward. If there are still areas that are uncertain or unclear...find out more information before you move forward. For example, if your dating period is ramping up to being engaged, you need full financial disclosure. Many people think this is being "nosy" and I agree that it is. But I explain they need to know what their "nose" is going to be exposed to when they get married. (Prov 20:11; Matt 7:20, 12:33)

3- Trust God's Word...it is your lifeline for guarding your heart as He instincts you to so that you can live the life He planned for you. Remember this: there is no situation that God's love can't overcome, break down, or completely replace. But God will not force you to receive His love...He respects your "no". I love going though the book of Proverbs in counseling and mentoring sessions with people when they are feeling like they are being "mean". There are numerous Proverbs we can reference to help us establish healthy boundaries in relationships because there's no missing what God instructs us to do. One of my favorites is Proverbs 19:19: "A hot tempered person must pay the penalty; rescue them, and you will have to do it again." To me this is crystal clear, yet many spend a lifetime trying not to upset the hot-tempered person or cleaning up their messes. But all they're doing is enabling the negative character patterns of the hot-tempered person, while forfeiting the individual plans God made for them long ago. (Pr 22:4, 27:12: Heb 6:18)

"The prudent person foresees danger and takes precautions. The simpleton goes blindly on and suffers the consequences." (Proverbs 22:3). Will you commit to seeking God and His people who are equipped to help you establish healthy boundaries? ♥LMM

2. On my last nerve…

*"If any of you lacks wisdom, you should ask God,
who gives generously to all without finding fault,
and it will be given to you."*

James 1:5 (NIV)

Let's be real. All of us have "discussions" about the "people" who push our buttons. They are the difficult personality types; we have to work really hard to redirect our thoughts and actions…you know what I'm talking about, right?

But if someone is getting on our nerves *it's our problem, not their problem.* This is good news because we can't control how a person acts toward us, but we can control how we respond to them. Most people know this and I know it, too—I've been teaching boundaries for years, but it's still some of the hardest character work I do in my personal life. Establishing healthy boundaries with a difficult family member or a person who we work closely with who's controlling, demanding, self-centered, narcissistic, rude, obnoxious, reckless, passive, petty, lazy, or just lies like a dog all day long…is hard work!

Our natural response is to ignore them, but ignoring always brings out the worst in us because ignoring doesn't resolve anything. Ignoring just holds back our undesired responses until we can't hold them back anymore and then…they pop out like a jack-in-the-box! The next thing we know, we are entertaining how much we want to punch them or for them to move a million miles away! Of course, neither of these responses is mature or realistic.

Our best response is to develop a plan that we're working through *before* someone gets on our last nerve. This enables us to take responsibility for what's in our heart and exercise the freedom God gives us to choose how we respond in every difficult situation.

Here are three things we can control:

1- Take ownership of our negative emotions by being real about how we feel. A lot of people get stuck here and deny their emotions because they feel wrong or bad for feeling the way they do. But how we feel is...how we feel. Taking ownership of our feelings opens the door for God's power to enable us to work through how we feel. (Phil 2:12-13)

2- Acknowledge the reality that a person's actions have the power to negatively impact us, but we can exercise the power God enables us in *how we choose to respond*. Many get stuck in wanting to "prove" how the person is wrong, but we gain no personal ground, we only exhaust ourselves in the process. We gain ground when we seek God's help because He will show us how their behavior is affecting our heart and give us wisdom for how to move forward. (James 1:5)

3- Finally, what we bring in the light...loses its power. Admitting our helplessness to God and asking for help from His people empowers us to face difficult situations. It's a supernatural process; God's power is perfected in our weaknesses and

His love pours through us individually and through His people and into our hearts when we're vulnerable and humbly open up our heart. (Eph 4:14-15; 2 Cor 6:13, 12:9)

Taking ownership for what's in our heart and establishing healthy boundaries is some of the hardest character work we will ever do, but we are promised a good return on our investment! Is anybody getting on your nerves today? ❤LMM

3. Stop trying to do God's job...you will lose your mind!

*"I can do everything through Christ,
who gives me strength."*

Philippians 4:13 (NLT)

Stop trying to do God's job...you will lose your mind. You're trying to fix impossible situations with human solutions! God strengthens us to do all things that He calls us to do...not what we call ourselves to do and then pray He backs us up. Our tendency is to tack Philippians 4:13 onto the end of our desire so that we can successfully carry it out. Although our intent may be sincere in desiring to carry out a good cause for God, if God didn't call us to the cause...the cause isn't going to do much good (yikes–that hurt). Does this make sense?

The real issue going on when someone is trying to do God's job is related to self-sufficiency coping skills. Self-sufficiency coping skills are usually rooted in early trust injures. Somewhere during a child's development they had to begin to rely on themselves instead of the adults in the home. This happens for numerous reasons like: negligence, abandonment, addictions, disease, and trauma. When a child is faced with not being able to consistently rely on an adult they do what is instinctive to protect themselves–in this situation they become self-reliant.

The coping skills that we used to protect us as a child are the same skills that disconnect us as an adult. In this situation, the coping skills of self-sufficiency in childhood met the need the parents were not meeting, but now the same skills in adulthood are keeping us from relying on God's sufficiency for a stable mind and emotional balance. For us to begin to transition from self-sufficiency to God-sufficiency, we will need to ask God to help us in these three areas:

1- God gives wisdom generously, but He usually doesn't give all the details we want, and *that's the part we don't like*. But our response to His wisdom determines the disposition of our heart– we will resort to human solutions, which *shut* the door on God's provisions, or we will rely on God's wisdom, which *opens* the door to His provisions. (James 1:5; Prov 3:4-5, 14:12)

2- With God we can do all things...apart from Him we can do nothing–that really means *nothing*. Most of us eventually get to a point where we're exhausted from trying to do God's job and in our own brokenness we submit to Him. When we do, we open the door for His love and grace to go to work through us and in the situations we're facing. "If you remain in me and I in you, you will bear much fruit; apart from me you can do nothing." (John 15:5; Eph 3:20; Phil 4:13)

3- There's no human solution for an impossible situation, but God's sufficiency promises to make a way when we turn to Him. His sufficiency is in the supernatural power of His love that's made perfect in our weaknesses–every time we take the risk to trust Him, we strengthen our trust in Him and break down our self-sufficiency. "I pray that the eyes of your heart may be enlightened in order that you may know the hope to which he has called you..." (Eph 1:18; 1 Cor 2:5; Mt 6:33)

Trying to do God's job will make us lose our mind. Will you open your mind and heart to His love and grace so that you can rely on His sufficiency instead of yours? ❤LMM

4. Different face...same place

"Trust in the Lord with all your heart and lean not on your own understanding; in all your ways submit to him, and he will make your paths straight."

Proverbs 3:5-6 (NLT)

Have you ever said, "I don't have to take this anymore"? It usually means you're fed up with a person or situation that's emotionally exhausting you. But saying, "I don't have to take this anymore" doesn't fix why you took it in the first place. Until we have an understanding into the reasons we keep "taking" certain situations to the point of emotional exhaustion...we will continue to find ourselves with the same kind of people in the same kind of emotionally exhausting situations. Many people understand in their head the boundary they need to establish with people who are emotionally exhausting them, but they aren't able to execute the boundary from within their heart because— they are flooded with an overwhelming emotional responsibility for the feelings and actions of the other person.

Our inability to execute heathy boundaries is driven by negative patterns of relating that we learned in relationships during our formative years. These negative patterns are rooted in a false sense of responsibility for others—*we make decisions based on how others feel and act towards us instead of our individual responsibility to guard our heart.* Our learned reasoning undermines the wisdom God gives us and subsequently we cannot execute the needed boundaries to guard our heart in a heathy way.

Due to our inability to execute healthy boundaries, we become emotionally exhausted. We believe leaving the relationship will solve our problem. Inevitably we begin a new one with the belief that things will be better. And things are better at first, but eventually the same old ways of relating emerge because...we repeat our patterns of relating until we learn new patterns of relating. I call this syndrome of changing relationships without changing patterns, "different face–same place". The faces change, but the same dynamic of relating remains the same...and the patterns perpetuate.

To stop our negative patterns of relating, we need God's wisdom, understanding of what beliefs in our heart drives them, and His people who have the insight and skills to help us learn healthy boundaries. Here are three steps that will get you started on the right path:

1- Entrust our heart to God's wisdom while asking Him to help us open up our heart to healthy relationships with His people. It's very vulnerable to receive without giving back and it is the reason that most resist– we prefer to be in control and give. (Prov 2:2-4, 4:5, 18:15)

2- To replace the old patterns of relating, we need a cognitive understanding of the negative patterns we internalized during our formative years, but this understanding does not replace the emotional experiences we need to learn how to change them. We need safe settings where we can experience being loved for who we are, not what we do– and to distinguish healthy love from the bad love of enabling and rescuing others. (Mk 7:8; Eph 1:18; Prov 28:26)

3- Be committed to a life and community of godly people who yield to the guidance of the Holy Spirit, give grace, and speak truth as a way of life so that you grow in God's love and establish healthy boundaries until you take your last breath. (John 16:13; Eph 4:21-25)

Are you ready to trust the Lord and not lean on your own understanding to change these negative patterns of relating? ❤LMM

5. Love covers...it doesn't deny

"Above all, love each other deeply, because love covers over a multitude of sins."

1 Peter 4:9 (NIV)

Many people come to counseling with heavy hearts —they want godly counsel in dealing with their loved ones' negative behaviors like: knowing how to verbalize needs in the marriage, setting boundaries with a rebellious teen, establishing financial limits on a spouse's overspending, asking an adult child to move out, dealing with an affair, or developing an intervention for an alcoholic spouse, etc. They are fearful that any kind of confrontation will cause more conflict in the relationship and push the person further into a path of destruction...*but it's when we don't speak truth that we cause more problems*!

Love covers a multitude of sins, but *covering doesn't deny*. Denying is the ultimate death of a relationship because truth is cut off and *truth is our life source*. We do not have the power to change each other, but we do have a responsibility to speak truth to each other. Jesus always spoke truth, but He rooted it in grace so it could be received, then He let time run its course for the undesired behavior to catch up with the heart changes. But many have settled for "keeping the peace" and hoping things will change. Both responses are counterfeit and unbiblical. Authentic peace creates conflict because it requires people to take a stand. And authentic hope isn't a cross-your-fingers kind of hope...it's the hope that raised Jesus from the dead!

Developing truthful relationships is some of the hardest work we will do in life this side of Heaven, but the hard work pales in comparison to the richness that comes with relationships that are rooted in God's truth. God's love gives us the courage to address sensitive issues in truth. When we love the way God designed for us to, we can authentically connect in truth, while addressing and moving through difficult issues. But we don't like addressing difficult issues because confrontation is uncomfortable; it always opens the door to increased conflict and rejection from the person being confronted. But if we give into our discomfort and fear of being rejected, we forgo the potential love, growth, and development in our relationships.

Here are three emotional disclaimers to explain why it is so difficult to confront in love:

1- When a person feels a false sense of responsibility for others they do not have the ability to confront in love. They understand the logic behind what they need to do, but they do not possess the defined boundaries in their heart to carry out what they need to do. (1 John 4:18; Acts 24:16; Ps 25:4)

2- The insult to injury of a person not being able to confront in love...*makes them a silent accomplice in the destruction of the relationship*. When I explain this to clients, it's an emotional punch in the gut, but it also propels them into action to heal their boundary deficit that feeds into the destruction of the relationship. (Hos 4:6; Phil 1:9-10; Ps 143:10; 1 Thess 5:11)

3- Authentic love is willing to go the extra miles of being uncomfortable and rejected in order to throw a lifeline to those who are in denial of the behaviors that are causing harm and creating problems in their life. None of us is exempt from denial; we have to constantly recalibrate our love to God's truth and be open to the loving instruction and correction from the the Body of Christ. (Ps 19:12, 25:5, 139:24)

Loving confrontation hurts and humbles us, but it never harms us– it's some of the best love we'll we will ever give or get because it prevents losing a life to denial. Love covers–it doesn't deny...are you loving or denying? ❤LMM

6. We don't pray away problems...we pray through problems

"If another believer sins against you, go privately and point out the offense. If the other person listens and confesses it, you have won that person back. But if you are unsuccessful, take one or two others with you and go back again, so that everything you say may be confirmed by two or three witnesses."

Matthew 18:15-16 (NLT)

Abuse and addictions have to be brought in the light and dealt with in a setting with people who are trained and licensed to help. Many families hide the abuse and addictions of their loved ones due to the fear of their family being judged and labeled. But when families try to handle these situations alone and behind closed doors, the situations only get worse by making the family emotionally sick. We are as sick as the secrets we keep. *What we hide in our heart will steal, kill, and destroy every promise God's made to us, but what we bring in the light, loses its power*.

We can't convince or make people take responsibility for their behavior, but we can choose how we will respond to their resistance to responsibility. The healthy boundary is to stop enabling their irresponsible behavior and/or exposing ourselves to it. Many are sincere in praying for the family member who is abusing and using, but we don't *pray away* problems...we *pray through* them. Praying through enables God to guide us in the wisdom for how to proceed in getting the help they/we need. If we are helping a person hide a behavior that causes harm to themselves and/or others, we are a silent accomplice in their sin and we are perpetuating evil in our home. Much of my practice is helping adults who were raised in homes with abuse and addictions–they are incredibly insecure and have difficulty establishing healthy boundaries in their relationships as they are growing up...patterns of generational sin perpetuate until the patterns are stopped.

If they don't get help, we still can, especially when children are involved. Until a person who is abusing others or medicating through substances has to face consequences, they won't–they can't. The harmful way they are treating people is a byproduct of the real problem–in their heart where they learned long ago a false solution for their pain. The abuse and substance use will always be their default behavior until they are in a setting with professionals who can walk them through their old pain and help them integrate the part of their heart that keeps them from getting the love they need.

Here are three straightforward steps and interventions for establishing boundaries in the home:

1- Humbly seek God for guidance and wisdom while opening up your heart to your pastor, a counselor, process therapy group, and or trusted friends who love, stand with, and pray with and for you. (James 1:5; Prov 15:22; Eph 5:13)

2- Seek individual counseling to establish personal boundaries– most likely you are perpetuating the unhealthy ways of relating from your family of origin. Don't allow guilt to distract you; none of us is perfect–*but when we know better, we do better*. God does not endorse any kind of violation of His children; we are His masterpieces. You are responsible to protect yourself and the children He's entrusted to you. He will empower you when you look to His grace and truth–what we bring in the light...loses its power! (Eph 2:10, 5:13; John 10:10)

3- Everybody in the family needs counseling to unlearn the denying, enabling, and negative ways of relating. Counseling does take time, but the time is an investment in the family and the empowering of future generations in overcoming destructive patterns of relating that have been morphing forward from previous generations. Every second of investment reaps a return on reversing the harm imposed on your family from all the yesterdays, todays, and tomorrows! (Prov 15:22; Lam 5:7; Gal 6:9)

Will you commit to praying through to enable God to guide you in the wisdom on how to proceed in getting the help that you and your loved one need? ❤LMM

7. We are as sick as the secrets we keep...

*"Then they will come to their senses and escape
from the devil's trap. For they have been held
captive by him to do whatever he wants."*

2 Timothy 2:26 (NLT)

Have you ever kept a secret about yourself or someone else? I'm talking about the kind of secrets where something bad happened to you or someone else or you made a choice you regretted, but you promised to keep what happened a secret. If so, you know the energy and emotional toll it takes to keep secrets. People keep secrets believing they are protecting others, but secrets always perpetuate problems for the people involved and for future generations. God made our mind, heart, and spirit to speak truth and life–not to hide or hold toxic secrets. Secrets make us sick– that's why the old saying is true: "we are as sick as the secrets we keep".

I've heard a lot of secrets over the years. With the help of the Holy Spirit and a safe setting, people are able to speak the secrets that were locked away for years in their heart. As the locked-up words come out of their mouth–waves of emotions come too...there's an explosion of hurt, anger, regret, sadness, and hope. But it's also the beginning of healing for carrying a burden that should never have been carried. If you've been carrying a secret that's made you sick, you do not have to carry it anymore.

Here's what you need to know and the choices you have:

1- People who've been carrying secrets need compassion and understanding. Many people make ignorant remarks about others and the reason they keep secrets. But the biggest insult to injury of carrying a toxic secret is: most people know they need to tell, but they don't know *how to*. And they don't know *how to* because the secret they're carrying is one that crossed the holy lines of their mind, body, and spirit. When this happens, a person's identity is dismantled and distorted–they don't know where they begin and end, or what they are or are not responsible for. They learned at an early age that their needs were not important, their voice was not heard, and if anybody would listen, they wouldn't be believed. (Eph 5:13-14,)

2- Secrets make every person involved sick and the devil has free reign to every person's heart who's hiding or holding onto a secret. Hiding or holding onto the secret, holds us hostage in the dark... but *what we bring in the light loses its power*! When we submit to God and His light of truth, the devil has to flee. God will help us find people who are equipped to walk us through the pain surrounding our secrets. (1 Ptr 4:8; Prov 28:26; James 4:6-8)

3- Don't underestimate the power of God's ability to connect you to the help you need! I am forever in awe of God's loving hand guiding and connecting people to the help they need to be healed. I've witnessed many miracles over the years. God is our only Source, but in the blink of an eye, He has access to a gazillion resources. So if you're carrying a secret, go to God

He. Will. Help.

"Those who look to him for help will be radiant with joy; no shadow of shame will darken their faces." (Ps 34:4)

I pray if you are keeping a secret, you will ask the Holy Spirit to give you the courage to bring it in the light with people who can help you handle it. Then the secret will no longer be allowed to steal, kill, and destroy the life Jesus came to give you! (John 10:10) ❤LMM

8. Boundary. Is. Not. A. Bad. Word.

"For we are each responsible for our own conduct."

Galatians 6:5 (NIV)

At the end of the day, if we keep finding ourselves worn out because a person is controlling our love, choices, feelings, and/or actions...*they* are not our problem. The problem is our inability to establish healthy boundaries. God gives us the final say—it's His design for us to guard our heart and take ownership for what's in it, so we can fulfill the purpose He put in us long ago. That's why

Boundary. Is. Not. A. Bad. Word.

Boundaries are God's design to help us know His truth and then walk in the freedom He promises us! I spend a lot of time helping my clients understand that their feelings are valid. Another person may have "caused them" to feel the way they do, but they are "responsible for" resolving the way they feel.

So here's the truth that hurts: nobody can make us do something we don't want to do—we choose how we want to respond. But if a person was not taught boundaries in their formative years, they believe they do not have a choice. But they do not have to stay stuck in this belief because God's truth has made a way.

Here are three steps that will begin to help a person put into practical application the truth God promises that will set us free for everyday life:

1- One of the hardest, but most life changing boundaries we can embrace in our heart and establish with others is: only we have the power to change ourself, not another person. Until we embrace this truth, we will spend a lifetime trying to "control" how others treat us. If you've ever tried to control how another person treats you, you know it's a losing fight. Yet many are stuck here because they think the other person is "their problem". So they go back into the ring only to be beaten to an emotional pulp. But the problem isn't that they are being beaten up...it's why they keep doing the same thing and expecting a different result–this is the definition of insanity! And apart from healthy boundaries...our lives are insane. (Rom 14:12; 2 Cor 5:10-11; Pr 14:10)

2- We can't carry out and sustain what we don't believe in our heart. One of the reasons many fail at establishing boundaries is they try to execute them based on their cognitive understanding. Boundaries are not rocket science–they are straightforward basic concepts that are understood by most people. We understand the concept of boundaries in our *head*, but to effectively execute them...we have to be in agreement with them in our *heart*. And it's in the heart where the contradictions live that oppose God's truth about boundaries. So when a person tries to execute the boundary they understand in their head, but their understanding is contradicted in their heart, they have a conflict of interest. They will not be able to carry out the boundary–their heart has the final say because it determines everything we do! But we're not tied to the lies that are ingrained in our heart. We can open up our heart to God's truth to be transformed. (Prov 4:23; Ps 26:2, 154:10)

3- Open up our heart to God's truth and His people to practice walking in agreement with the boundaries we want to execute. For that to happen, we have to have emotional heart surgery and dismantle the lies that oppose God's truth. This is a tedious and time consuming process that is complicated by other lies that are tangled up in the heart. My clients work hard, I work hard, and the Holy Spirit is hard at work doing an internal transformation in my clients' heart...pouring in God's grace while tearing down lies and taking responsibility for all the emotions involved. But it's worth the blood, sweat, and tears because God's truth sets them free to begin to walk in the freedom promised. (Jn 8:31-32,10:10; Eph 2:10)

We can't make another person stop a behavior towards us, but we can choose how we respond to them. Until we do, we relinquish the freedom God promises us into another person's hands...and that's a miserable way to live! Are you trying to control your behavior or the behavior of another person? ❤LMM

9. You are not being selfish when you take care of your needs…

"You're going to wear yourself out–and the people, too. This job is too heavy a burden for you to handle all by yourself."

Exodus 18:18 (NLT)

Do you ever feel like you're being pulled on all sides? No matter how hard you try and how much you set your mind to accomplishing what you plan to do, at the end of the day it's never enough. Then on top of not having enough time, do you struggle with taking care of yourself emotionally, physically, and spiritually? Finding the time seems impossible because– every new day brings a former "undone" one with it!!! If we're stuck in this rut, we will vacillate from being mad at God, to feeling God is mad at us for letting Him down, to resenting others for all they need, to feelings of self-loathing for what we haven't done. Many make attempts to manage their schedules better, but they often feel they are being selfish in some way because someone doesn't get what they need or something goes undone. So how does a person choose one important thing over another???

Well, for starters, you need to know you're not alone in how you feel. This is a common struggle that I help people work through; it's also something I'm constantly working through in my personal life. God designed us to experience fulfillment in work, but He never intended for us to deny the emotional needs He put in us, or try to do His job! When we are responsible in taking care of our needs, we're good at giving others what they need. But if we have an emotional boundary deficit in this area, we will struggle to distinguish what is reasonable, sustainable, and impossible to do.

Here are three truths to get started–most know these truths, but *knowing* the truth isn't our problem...it's how we *respond* to the truth that's our problem. And how we respond is found in our heart, where we learned about boundaries long ago. What we learned is our point of reference and it will always trump what we desire. That's why we can't make boundary changes apart from God and His people. So when you begin to incorporate these truths, seek God first, ask His people for help, and take them slow and one step at a time.

1- Be reasonable; God's not shocked by our struggles. If we are–we're thinking too highly of ourselves. God made us with needs; we have to ask God and people for our needs to be met. When we seek and ask for help, we are being responsible stewards of our heart and life. God's instruction is very clear to us: He tells us to guard our heart above all else because it determines everything we do. But the problem is that many people were not taught reasonable responsibility (healthy boundaries) during their formative years, they were taught a false sense of responsibility where they feel responsible for people's feelings, decisions, behaviors, obligations, chores, etc.

Many understand the concept of boundaries; they are basically straightforward. But it's the emotional unraveling and understanding the messages that were written on the tablet of our heart that overrides us not being reasonable and feeing a false sense of responsibility for others. Until we connect these dots, we will default to what we know instead of what we need to do because our heart determines everything we do! (Prov 4:23; Rom 12:13; Num 11:14, 17)

2- Determine what is sustainable; we are not being selfish when we take care of our needs before others. To be a good *giver*–we have to be a good *receiver*. God put the same set of emotional needs in every person. We need to protect our boundary lines...knowing where our responsibility begins and ends. When we ask for and receive *our* needs being met, we have the emotional capacity to meet the needs of *others* in a healthy way. If we ignore our needs, we will be emotionally depleted and directly disobedient.

The trap many get stuck in is the justification that they are doing something good and that others are relying on them. But if what we're doing is pushing us beyond our resources and depleting us emotionally, physically, or spiritually then our good is no longer good because we are burning out and unable to sustain. God wired our body to signal us when we are hungry, angry, lonely, and tired. But if we weren't taught to listen to our body, we won't know how to trust what we hear. Not trusting what we hear places us in danger internally and externally. I'm going to add one more disclaimer to this scenario: some people *do* hear the signal their body gives and recognize the danger. They believe God can heal them, but they do not pursue resources He makes available through the Body of Christ– His people. Their belief is correct, but their understanding is distorted. God alone is our Source and He *can* heal us with one touch of His hand. But more often than not, God uses us, the Body of

Christ, as His main resource. The bottom line is don't forfeit God's help by boxing Him in with human understanding. (Prov 3:5-6, 9:6-7; Deut 1:9, 1:12; Exodus 18:17)

3- Accept reality; we can't do the impossible–that's God's job! Change is a process–it takes time, people, and most of all...it takes God! He's got us covered, *but we've got to let Him do His job*. But slowly, as we keep asking God to search our heart for the beliefs that oppose His truth, continue opening up and being vulnerable to the help He sends, and consistently put into practice what we're learning we will internalize God's truths into our heart to replace our former beliefs that opposed His truth. This is how we continue take care of our heart as God instructs us to while doing His work and not labor in vain. (1 Cor 12:20, 15:10, 15: 58; 2 Cor 3:2)

Many know these truths and understand them cognitively, but we need the practices listed above...the experiential process. These things *won't* change overnight, but we *will* see change because we're following God's blueprint for change. Are you ready to start asking for what you need? ❤LMM

10. The struggle is real…

"For we are God's masterpiece. He has created us anew in Christ Jesus, so we can do the good things he planned for us long ago."

Ephesians 2:10 (NLT)

Inside every human heart is the desire to be known deeply and completely– to know we matter, have a purpose, are accepted and loved at all times. God put this need in us. When we know this truth, it enables us to grow, develop, heal, and be our "real" self...the masterpiece God designed! This truth is confirmed in Ephesians 2:10, but we still struggle believing it at times– it's just part of being an imperfect human living in a messed up world. None of us are exempt from struggling–it is normal human behavior. But where the lines get blurred and abnormal behavior morphs is when struggle becomes a way of life–struggle becomes an *identity*. And when struggle becomes an identity, it undermines our "real" self–our identity in Christ. (2 Cor 5:17)

The biggie I see over and over in my practice where struggles become an identity is when people *try to convince themselves* into believing God's truth for their life apart from "owning the behavior that opposes God's truth" in their life. They profess Scripture and claim God's promises, but hardly anything changes because they reject responsibility for their choices, embrace false humility, and/or refuse the vulnerability required in getting help. Doing any one of these things denies ownership of our behaviors and stunts the development of our "real" self, which forfeits the good plans God made for us long ago.

If you feel like your struggles are becoming your identity—you don't have to settle for staying stuck one more day. You have options that will help you get on course. Here are three steps to get you going in the right direction:

1- Letting go of the defense, "I had to". When a person believes they "had to" make a decision that they didn't want to they forfeit their say in the outcome. This is an area where I have to go head-to-head in love to help clients take responsibility for their choices. The struggles we are dealing with may not be our *fault*..but they are our *responsibility*. It's hard to own our negative choices; we like to shift the blame and say: "the devil made me do it". An example would be a person who struggles with setting boundaries, but they are not in counseling working on the issue. They complain how the devil "always" makes them feel guilty if they try to say "no". *But the devil can't make them feel guilty about something that they don't already feel guilty about*! But he can sure beat them up emotionally in areas that they're struggling in, like this person is with boundaries.

The devil will go after the same weak spot every time because he gets results, but he only gets results because the "unhealed wound" already exists. When we blame our decision or situation on someone or something, we defer our outcome to the person or situation and forfeit the freedom we're promised to walk in. (John 8:32; Gen 3:12-13; Prov 3:5)

2- Embrace humility. Humility opens the door for our "real" self to develop and be in relationship as God designed. We learn to normalize struggle instead of being shocked when our weaknesses hold us back or when we mess up. Normalizing gives us permission to bring these things into relationship with God and others who can help us. God's not shocked at our weaknesses or messes, so we shouldn't be either. The belief that God is let down when we have weaknesses or messes is false humility. False humility is self-focused instead of God-focused. False humility keeps us stuck, but we don't have to stay there! Humbly ask God for His help– He gives wisdom without finding fault. He opposes the proud, but gives grace to the humble. (James 1:5, 4:6, 4:10)

3- Reaching out for help and joining a safe and structured setting like counseling, mentoring, or group process to practice being vulnerable and letting love in your heart. To say you will feel awkward is an understatement– the struggle is real!!! Until we can practice being vulnerable in a safe setting and *experience* opening up our heart, we will not know *how* to to be vulnerable.

Being vulnerable is key to being connected in relationships that connect and develop the "real" self. People who don't pursue this kind of structure and vulnerability will wish they could believe God's truth for their life, wish they had close friendships, and wish they didn't feel so overwhelmed with life, etc. We are responsible for asking for what we need...it's God's way to keep us vulnerable and on course for our "real" self to develop. (Matt 7:7; 2 Cor 7:2; Ruth 1:16)

If you find yourself in a perpetual state of struggle, I pray you won't settle and let it become your identity. The struggles are real, but staying stuck isn't the status quo for a saved person because the Lord has gone ahead of us and made a way (Psalm 135:5)! Will you reach out and ask for help or pass this information on to someone who needs it?
❤LMM

NOTES

Chapter Three

Integrating heart–
the chasm of contradiction

*"So now there is no condemnation for those who
belong to Christ Jesus."*

Romans 8:1 (NLT)

Our third stage of emotional development is integrating our heart…closing the chasm of contradiction. Every person has some issue in this stage because none of us have a perfectly integrated heart. First, we we're born with some sin (thanks, Adam and Eve). We have grandiose expectations that are impossible to meet, but when we don't meet them, we annihilate ourselves. And all this happens *before* we experience any emotional trauma! So, the sooner we can admit that we need a lot of help, the sooner we can cooperate with and embrace the unlimited amount of grace God so generously gives. But unlimited grace isn't to endorse us being a mess–unlimited grace accepts and loves us where we are so that we can

Love. And. Accept. Ourself.

When we've internalized grace in our significant relationships during our formative years, we're able to bring our bad, not good enough, and sinful parts of our heart into relationship and ask for the help we need. But many of us were criticized when we brought our real selves into relationship. We are at our greatest risk for strongholds to set up during this developmental stage because the part of our heart that's not invited into relationship will go into hiding and take on a separate life–and, if not healed, this is also the beginning stages of duplicity.

When we're growing up, we rely on the cues and guidance from the people in our early relationships to let us know how we are supposed to respond to the positive and negative things that come out of our heart. If we're met with grace, we internalize grace in our heart. If not, the judgement imposed on us is internalized as self-judgment. We become conditioned in watching the faces of people to measure our worth. This pattern of behavior isolates us in our own heart and it feels like hell on earth.

When we are young our emotions are ginormous and we need help handling them. One minute everything feels right and the next minute it's falling apart. Observe any two-year-old and you know exactly what I'm talking about, right? But a two-year-old who doesn't have someone helping him with his emotions is going to be an overwhelmed little guy who grows up to be an overwhelmed big man. When we're anxious, afraid, sad, mad, mean, struggling to learn our ABCs, heartbroken about the death of our favorite pet, or vacillating between hating and loving ourselves, our family, and everybody around us, and we are met with love and acceptance–then our heart comes together in one place to form one emotional home. This is what God's grace looks like on the inside of us….a place where both good and bad can live and be loved and accepted at the same time. His love and acceptance of our real self are critical in the healthy formation of our personality structure and character development.

None of us move through this stage without some kind of emotional injury because we are imperfect people being raised by imperfect people. But whatever emotional needs we missed, we still need them because...*growing up doesn't mean we outgrow our emotional needs*. We can't convince ourselves to believe the love and acceptance that we have not experienced. But when we bring the rejected, hidden, and shamed parts of our heart into relationship with God and His people, and we are accepted as we are...then we are going to heal. When we have enough grace on board in our heart, we're not shocked by what we're not. We can honestly look at and evaluate the parts of our heart that have sin, character flaws, and emotional injuries to make the necessary changes, but have patience, love, and acceptance for ourselves while we move through them.

Until we reconcile the reality that our unmet emotional need for grace has to be healed and is an ongoing daily fuel that we need in our close relationships our travel time to Heaven is going to be one very long, miserable, and incredibly disappointing ride. Like in the previous chapters, the symptom list below is information to help you, not overwhelm or discourage you, so before you go over it, ask the Holy Spirit to guard your heart. Apart form grace our heart will suffer with the following emotional and psychological issues: inability to admit faults, weaknesses or apologizing, denying bad parts, commitment issues, struggle with forgiving self, perfectionism, narcissism, optimism, idealism, fantasy, denial, shame, bulimia and distorted body image, sexual addiction, drug and alcohol abuse, anxiety, panic attacks, struggle with injustices and unfairness, and all good or all bad view.

The following 10 situations are examples that I see most often in my practice, how the unmet needs manifest when they go untreated, the symptoms most people experience, and the practical application that are rooted in biblical solutions to get us on the road to recovery. I pray as you read through this next chapter, you will ask the Holy Spirit to prepare your heart to begin to open up to the love and acceptance of His grace that He will pour through His people to begin your healing process...it's never too late. There's no expiration date on us experiencing God's grace through His people! ❤LMM

1. Will someone please…meet me in my pain???

"And why do you break the command of God for the sake of your tradition?"

Matthew 15:3 (NIV)

When we're all getting along life is good, but it's how we get along when things are going wrong… that tests what we really know about getting along. If you've ever been in a relationship where you keep having the same argument over and over—you know first-hand the meaning of emotional exhaustion…and it's a painful place to live! Many people eventually apologize, but if they don't have some understanding of the underlying dynamic that drives the argument, it's just a matter of time before the same argument happens again. And it's this same argument that is the ultimate painful death of a relationship. Until we have understanding of the underlying dynamic of an argument, we cannot reach a reasonable resolution.

Many simply settle instead of reaching a reasonable resolution in their relationship. Many continue to ride the pain emotional rollercoaster, others seek counseling but only focus on symptoms instead of root causes, so nothing changes. Others keep a counterfeit peace in between explosive arguments, and some file for divorce. All of these are heartbreaking choices.

The only way we know how to respond to conflict is the way it was modeled for us during our formative years; we default to the patterns of relating that we learned in our family of origin… especially during conflicts! There are many unhealthy models of relating, including pleasing, passivity, lying, leaving, fighting, retaliating, or "trying not to do" what the family of origin did, which isn't successful either. Most of the people I counsel genuinely desire to change the negative ways they relate during conflict. They cognitively understand that they have an unhealthy response to conflict, so they try really hard to continue to change the negative ways they relate. But their trying eventually comes to an end because their willpower gives out to the unknown underlying dynamic.

Change happens when we begin to gain understanding of how our negative ways of relating were written on our heart during our formative years. To make changes, we need experiences–actual clock hours of practicing that teach new ways of relating in response to conflict. The bottom line is until we learn new ways of relating we will default to what we know: the unhealthy ways that were ingrained in our hearts long ago.

Relationships *hurt us and heal us*–they tear us down and build us up; this is a reality of life. But our ability to relate in healthy ways is a requirement for being in healthy relationships. The good news is God wants us to relate in healthy ways in our relationships and He will help us until we take our last breath. Below are three non-negotiable truths needed in establishing healthy relationships God's way:

1- Reliance on the Holy Spirit: we can't grow and develop or change deeply ingrained patterns in our heart apart from the help of the Holy Spirit. The Holy Spirit is our full-time Helper. We need to be talking with Him constantly and asking for help in our struggles and strongholds. Be specific in what you're experiencing and what you need. For example, if you're in the middle of an argument and want to pull away and shut down...ask the Holy Spirit to empower you with the courage to establish healthy boundaries, speak truth in love, and stay connected when you want to run. (Rom 8:26; John 14:26; Ps 14:10)

2- Unconditional love: enables us to experience all the parts of our heart being loved–the good, bad, and ugly. Giving full disclosure of where we've been and what we've done and knowing we're accepted by God's grace from Him and His people is the model for love. It's the game-changer that empowers us to turn around, rise up, and move forward! When we're in a difficult relationship, we need extra unconditional love from other godly people to pour into us the love we're not getting in our relationship.

This love enables us to stand up and stay connected in the relationship while having the "maturity" to love the other person when they are not loving us. Taking this position to love the difficult person is by far one of the most deep character works we will do this side of Heaven! If this difficult relationship is a marriage, this extra unconditional love can save a marriage and turn it around. And this kind of love also empowers one to love from a physical distance if necessary if there is some form of abuse. This kind of "godly" love affirms and validates our heart to remain protected by people who are for us and our marriage, verses just talking to people about our marriage problems...which can justify affairs. (Rom 8:1; Eph 2:20, 3:16-20)

3- Complete honesty: blessed is the person who has someone who loves them enough to speak truth to the areas of their life that need change. God's truth is a lifeline and saves us from the enemy's traps! If you have a history of being in unhealthy relationships, you will need to unlearn the unhealthy ways of relating in "safe hands" with a Christian licensed counselor, counseling pastor, Bible-based process group, group therapy, organized retreats, or in an established group that meets on a regular basis. (Eph 4:25; James 5:20; Gal 6:1)

You do not have to settle—someone can meet you in your pain. Will you commit to actively engage in the above steps so that you can continue to grow and develop in the healthy ways of relating as God intended? ❤LMM

2. It takes guts to speak God's truth…

*"Whoever turns a sinner from the error of their way
will save them from death and cover over a
multitude of sins."*

James 5:20 (NIV)

It takes guts to speak God's truth to those we love
who are in sin, but God makes a way when we
partner with Him in truth! Many ignore sin in loved
ones for fear of pushing the person into more sinful
behavior. Listen closely: *if you were powerful
enough to push a person into sinful behavior…you
would be powerful enough to stop their sinful
behavior.* God calls us to be responsible in
delivering His truth—we're not responsible for how a
person responds to His truth…that's God's job.
Until sin is confronted in love restoration can't take
place.

We don't like to confront because confrontation is
uncomfortable. It always opens the door to conflict
and potential rejection of the relationship by the
person being confronted. But if we give into our
discomfort and fear of being rejected, we forgo the
potential for love, growth, and development in our
relationships. Love is willing to be uncomfortable
and rejected in order to throw a lifeline to those
who are in denial of the behaviors that are causing
harm and creating problems in their life. None of us
are exempt from denial; we have to constantly
recalibrate our love to God's truth and be open to
the loving input and correction from the the Body of
Christ. Loving confrontation hurts and humbles us,
but it never harms us—*it's some of the best love we*

will ever give or get because it prevents losing a life to denial!

These three insights will help you have the "guts" to speak God's truth to your loved ones:

1- Have difficult conversations; the enemy wants you to avoid difficult conversations. Avoidance resorts to a shallow relationship– the mentality is, "as long as you don't bring up my wrong we can get along!" Truth is the growth agent in healthy and authentic relationships–it's God's design! Without truth love can't grow and without love a relationship withers and dies. (Ps 85:10, 119:136; Rom 9:1)

2- The best defense...is a good offense. Know your weaknesses– the enemy does! The enemy will intimidate you in your areas of weakness by bombarding your mind with questions, potential scenarios, and your "Christian duty" to fix the person. Recognize the mental mind-trap that he's led you into. He's trying to get you to accept a false sense of responsibility for the the person. Don't accept responsibility for their behavior, but don't justify your position either. Instead, assert your right to guard your heart above all else and not be placed in a position that would compromise you emotionally, physically, financially, professionally, spiritually and so on. You *can't* change a person's behavior, but you *can* state what you will or will not do. (Prov 4:23; 2 Cor 2:4,2:9)

3- Confronting sin is an opportunity for restoration...turning a sinner from the error of their ways will save them from death and cover a multitude of sins! Ignoring a loved one's sin makes you a *silent accomplice* in their path of destruction!

God's truth is the mortar that seals an authentic relationship. His model for love requires us to have the guts to execute, carry out, and require truth as the standard by which we live. When we partner with God in truth…He makes a way! (James 1:22, 5:19-20; John 8:31-33)

God's love never fails us! Will you have the guts to speak God's truth in love to those you are in relationship with? ❤LMM

3. I'm trying to be your friend—but you won't let me…

"We are not withholding our affection from you, but you are withholding yours from us."

2 Corinthians 6:12 (NIV)

God put the need for belonging inside of every human heart. We need to belong to someone and something bigger than ourselves. Our birth family is where we are supposed to have our first experiences in belonging. Knowing we belong in relationships during our early years enables us to feel secure in relationships during our later years. But God knows this plan doesn't always work out. If we didn't experience the belonging we needed during our early years, God promises to place us in a new family where we belong to someone and something bigger than ourselves. That new family is the Body of Christ, His church—that's *us*…His people.

The church is where we're supposed to connect to the Body of Christ, but it's where many go through the motions and hide their lonely and hurting heart. *Many people are deeply committed to their church, but not deeply connected to God's people*. Week after week and sometimes for years, people stand shoulder-to-shoulder, but they don't know what's going on deep in the heart of those they're standing beside. There's a genuine concern for each other, ongoing prayer, and updates, but there's not a vulnerable opening-up of the heart, where grace can fill the place of isolation in our heart, so it can heal as God designed.

Until we open up and let others see the hidden and vulnerable parts of our heart and then experience their warmth, empathy, and unconditional acceptance...we will forfeit the belonging we're promised. God sends the transforming power of grace through His people to help and heal our heart. The problem is most won't allow others to come into the hidden parts of their hearts. Their position is understandable because they've been hurt, but their way perpetuates isolation and leads to further loneliness instead of toward the belonging they need from God and His people.

For a person to begin to work through feelings of not belonging and isolation in their heart, they will need to embrace these three truths so that healing can begin:

1- Volunteering is valued, but it doesn't *replace* intimate connection–*being close in physical proximity doesn't qualify as emotional intimacy.* I know all kinds of wonderful, caring, helpful people who have been actively involved in church most of their adult life, but they do not have the deep, abiding, intimate connections in their heart that transform our life when we know that we belong. To know this belonging that God promises us, we have to move beyond the Sunday experience and get involved in one-on-one connection in mentor settings, structured Bible study groups where individuals share and process feelings, retreats focused on vulnerability and growth, or Christian individual therapy. These types of settings are specifically structured and safe for people to open up their heart to the intimacy needed to experience the healing God promises. (Eph 4:1,6; Proc 16:25; 1 Ptr 4:8)

2- Be purposed in responding to potential friendships– the affection of those who reach out to you. There's always a risk of being hurt, but it pales in comparison to the potentially deep connections that can take place. God is forever sending help; it's our responsibility to respond. (2 Cor 6:11, 7:2; Prov 17:17; Ps 68:6)

3- Accept the truth that belonging is an emotional need that God put in our hearts. If we do not pursue the path He provides for us to experience and open up our hearts to be known…we will feel like we do not belong, and will remain lonely no matter how many people profess their love and acceptance of us. The essence of our existence is to belong and to be in relationship. We can't provide that for ourselves; we have to be vulnerable and open up our heart to relationships. It is in intimate relationships that we are rooted and grounded in God's love and the love of His people, and then we know that we belong. (Eph 3:17; Col 2:7; 1 Cor 3:9)

God sends us friends so we can experience the need of belonging and relationship– a good friend loves at all times. Will you open up your heart to the people who are trying to be your friend? ❤LMM

4. I just didn't want to bother anyone…

"Stay alert! Watch out for your great enemy, the devil. He prowls around like a roaring lion, looking for someone to devour."

1 Peter 5:8 (NIV)

Have you ever been in a bad situation and wondered how it got so bad? That realization can be sobering—bad situations have a million faces: rebellious teenager, failing marriage, financial troubles, career failures, sexual addiction, hidden gambling debt, depression, alcohol and drug abuse, eating disorders, estranged relationships, duplicitous lifestyle, and on and on. When we're facing a bad situation, the first thing we need to do is call on the name of Jesus and ask for help from His people.

I can't tell you how many bad situations I've listened to over the years for which people didn't ask for help. When I ask why they didn't, they respond with: "I didn't want to bother anyone." Our tendency is to not want to bother anyone. But that kind of thinking opens the door for the enemy to separate and isolate us from the *comfort, clarity, and connection* that we need during bad situations in life.

The enemy knows our weaknesses—so he patiently waits and watches for us to be in our weakest moments to devour us! Many believe the enemy's trap is to get us to do bad things that morph into bad situations—and certainly this is part of his agenda, but his motives are much more sinister than getting us to do bad things. The enemy's ultimate scheme is to keep us separated and isolated from relationships by challenging our motives for needing help, and having us believe that we are bothering people and that we are immature if we ask. But he's a liar! God created us to need Him and each other, to be connected to Him and each other through His Son, Jesus. This connection is our lifeline to:

- prevent a bad situation
- go through a bad situation
- recover from a bad situation

When we're *separated and isolated* from relationship it is likened to hell. We're cut off from the comfort, clarity, and connection that we need to survive and thrive! If we're saved the enemy can't take us to hell, so the next best thing he can do is have us to "feel like" we're living in hell by luring us away from the relationships we need.

Here are three subtle ways the enemy lures us away from relationships and isolates us from the help we need. To do this, he will:

1- Challenge the validity of our needs—this is the first line of attack in the enemy's schemes. He challenges whether our need is valid or not. But *validity is not the issue...need is the issue and comfort is the answer.* God designed us with needs. We cannot meet our own needs and we cannot comfort ourselves apart from the comfort we internalize from God and through His people. So we have to be humble and ask for what we need—taking responsibility for what we need aligns ourself with God's help.

When we have the confidence of God being for us and His people standing with us we can *stand up and be rooted in love* to face bad situations and possibly prevent them from developing. None of us are ever at a place in our growth and development where we will not have needs. Our needs don't go away when we minimize or ignore them– they are met when we do things God's way. But if we believe our needs are invalid or that we should just ignore them, we are thinking exactly how the enemy wants us to think and we will not reach out and ask for what we need, which will forfeit the help God and His people will give. (Col 2:8; Eph 3:17-19; Ps 34:9)

2- Challenge our need for help as bothering someone–this is the enemy's second level of scheming, where he will completely annihilate our thoughts and create confusion in our minds. But, the issue isn't whether or not we should or should not bother. The issue is why do we believe that we are bothering someone when we need help? Believing we are bothering someone separates us from the clarity God will give us and perpetuates the fear in our heart that we feel when we're in the middle of a bad situation.

Anytime we're experiencing fear, our thoughts will diminish because our thought processes are secondary to our emotional processes. We need clarity during these times and *God will give but we must take responsibility and ask for it*. We are never too far gone to turn around to receive the clarity that God will give us during bad situations. (John 17:22-24; Isa 26:3; Ps 18:6)

3- Challenge our walk with God as being immature. This is the enemy's third level of scheming where he will close us off in isolation. Expressing our needs and submitting to God is actually a sign of maturity. Our submission opens the floodgates of God's grace. And it's God's grace that will connect us with Him and catapult us through and onto the other side of a bad situation! Apart from it we are left in isolation with no help or hope for the future. The sooner we embrace God's grace the sooner we can get the help we need to turn around. (Prov 2:10; James 4:6-7; 2 Cor 10:5)

When we humble ourself before God the devil has to flee! Will you ask for help when you need it… especially when you're facing a bad situation? I pray that you do. ❤LMM

5. Dismantling distortions...

"We demolish arguments and every pretension that sets itself up against the knowledge of God, and we take captive every thought to make it obedient to Christ."

2 Corinthians 10:5 (NIV)

Our view of ourself, others, God, and the world in general is formed in the context of our early relationships, before we have the ability to reason or process thoughts. These early relationships tell us "who we are" and then we internalize the messages and write them on our heart as a point of reference. If our point of reference lines up with God's truth and who He says we are, we're off to a good start in life. But for most, this good start is not a reality. Most experience emotional isolation where safety, trust, and sense of belonging were not met. This reality would be daunting and steal any cause for hope, but ,thank you, Jesus, we're not stuck with the harsh realities imposed on us—we live in redeemed time and Jesus is our Redeemer! We do not have to grope in the dark for answers. Through His grace we can still get what we missed in our early development. Now is the time to say, "Amen"!

Our emotional development is created by God, so when we have an emotional development issue, it's in His Word where we can find the answer. Our emotional development is primary and our thought processes are secondary, so if our emotional foundation is unstable—our thoughts are unstable. If are emotions are unstable, our thoughts do not have have a stable place to root into and *unstable thoughts morph into distortions*.

To dismantle these distortions, we have to seek God and take responsibility for committing to work on resolving the distortions, model God's design for relationship, and have a basic understanding of how distortions originate, as explained in the following three steps:

1- Responsibility for distortions; Seek God. This step seems easy enough, but people get stuck in repressing distortions and denying them instead of bringing them in the light of God's truth and taking responsibility for them. For example, a person will profess Scripture like Ephesians 2:10 and say they are "God's masterpiece", which is true, but if the person does not name the distortion or have insight into why they do not believe that they are God's masterpiece…then they will default back to what they believe. Our first step in taking responsibility in dismantling our distortions always begins with seeking God. When we humble ourselves before Him and ask Him to search our hearts, He will give us His grace, wisdom, and people to help. (James 4:9-10; Ps 139:23-24; 2 Cor 1:4)

2- Rules learned in relationships are the origin of distortions; our ability to recognize that our distortions originated during our formative years in our significant relationships enables us to understand many of the underlying dynamics that drive them today. Until we understand the origin, we aren't able to distinguish and sort out our feelings from back then and now. For example, if a husband had a critical mother, he will project his unresolved mother issues onto his wife when she asks him a valid question. Instead, of hearing her question as a means to better *understand* what he's doing he will hear her being *critical* about what he's doing. Unresolved hurt skews our view of living in the present because our thoughts and actions operate from the perspective of past pain. Until the husband understands this, his attempts to correct his distortions will be unsuccessful. (Ps 40:11, 139:23-24, 143:10)

3- Realize distortions are rooted in our view of ourselves, others, and God. Once a client has insight into their relational skill of projecting their past pain onto others in relationships, they can connect the origin of their distortion and the subsequent thought patterns. I draw and graph their thought patterns on the whiteboard so that they have a visual reference for what they are hearing in their head, and a point of reference for what they are emotionally experiencing. Then they are equipped to interrupt the pattern when it happens. (Prov 2:6; Ps 51:6; Rom 9:1)

God's Word is true and it doesn't return void, but it doesn't negate the reality that we can't move on from what we haven't worked through. Will you take ownership to dismantle the distortions that are undermining God's promises in your life? ❤LMM

6. Why do I do…what I don't want to do???

*"I don't really understand myself, for I want to do
what is right, but I don't do it.
Instead, I do what I hate."*

Romans 7:15 (NLT)

Romans 7:15 is a heart cry that every one of us can relate to, right? And it's the defeated cycle that many are in when they come in for an initial session with me. They have been diligent in setting their minds on saying "no" to the undesired behavior they want to stop, and they have memorized Scripture and are taking authority in the name of Jesus, but all their *sincere trying doesn't stop them from slipping into the behaviors they despise in themselves*! They are sad, mad, and discouraged. Even though this is such a discouraging place to be, I explain it's a place full of potential and hope… what??? I know, it sounds crazy, but it's when we are the most depleted that we are the most open to help and change—and this is where I have the opportunity to work with people.

I spend a lot of time helping people process and understand the reasons that saying "no" to undesired behavior and quoting Scripture isn't enough to lead and keep them in victory. We do need to say "no" and we do need to speak God's Word—there is power in the name of Jesus! But God instructs us to do more than speak His word, He wants us to *rely on Him and reach out to His people* for comfort and connection. Until a person embraces this truth, they will continue to rely on their willpower and promise God, themselves, and others that this time will be different. But it's not; it's just like the last time...they try harder and keep saying "no" but "no" is never enough to stop the:

- overspending
- lying
- porn
- hopelessness
- rage
- gambling
- affairs
- binge eating
- alcohol/drugs
- broken promises
- anxious thoughts
- guilty feelings
- destructive relationships
- hopelessness
- etc.

It's not easy for any of us to open up—especially if we've been hurt in relationships. But the acceptance that we turn away from is the very acceptance that we need to turn around! When we humble ourselves before God and bring all of the "hidden" parts of our heart into relationship with Him and His people, we are promised His grace to heal!

Here's what we must do to begin to get a grip on the behavior that we don't want to do:

1- Making up our mind to change is the first step to changing— it's a decision of our conscious will, *but our conscious will by itself doesn't have the power to independently make changes to the rest of our being*. We have to bring all of ourselves into relationship with God— all of our heart, all of our soul, all of our strength, and all of our mind...all of our entire being into the change process. (Luke 10:27; Isa 55:11; James 5:6)

2- The desires of our heart, both good and bad, drive our behaviors– they determine everything we do. It's natural for us to oppress or deny the parts of our heart that we are ashamed of or fear will be judged. But until we bring these parts in the light before God and His people who can help us, we rely on our willpower and conscious will…and both fail us miserably! *No person has ever saved themselves with willpower*. And our conscious will doesn't have a chance against the the things we don't want to do because our *desires will override our conscious will, drive our behavior, and dominate our lives*! (Matt 15:8; Ps 26:2; Eph 1:18)

3- We need to intimately know, study, memorize, and profess God's Word–it is full of power and will not return void. But God's Word can't change the parts of our heart that we hold back or hide from relationship. Most share with God but they don't share with His people. His people is "us". We are here for a huge reason: we are God's manifolds of grace. God pours His grace through us to unconditionally accept and love each other. Letting others in our heart to see our messes is one of the most vulnerable and life-changing things we will ever do apart from giving our life to Christ. When we tell someone about all of the stuff we've been holding back and hiding in our heart and they look into our eyes and tell us that they love and accept us–the power of God's transforming grace goes to work inside of us. This power is the same power that raised Jesus from the dead! (1 Cor 15:10; 2 Cor 3:5; Phil 2:13)

Will you humble yourself before God, ask Him to search your heart and reveal what's undermining His good plans for your life, and then seek His people who are equipped to help you walk out the purpose He put in you? ♥LMM

7. Back in the pit again…

"Oh, what a miserable person I am! Who will free me from this life that is dominated by sin and death?"

Romans 7:24 (NLT)

You're back in the same pit you swore you'd never be again—you despise yourself for being here, but here you are. You've climbed out many times, but this time you're done. You're mad, sad, and embarrassed—you feel like you could explode! You asked a bunch of people to pray for you...but the thought of facing them is unbearable. Guilt is going down the list and reminding you of every failure while shame is screaming:

You. Are. A. Failure!

And this is exactly the hopeless place in the pit where the enemy wants you to stay! You're not alone, we all have a personal pit of some kind: addictions, obsessive-compulsive behaviors, psychological issues, character flaws, and distorted thinking, etc. Most people spend their life trying to stop these behaviors to stay out of the pit. This response seems like logical, but this logic sends them right back to the pit. And this is why they feel so confused and hopeless. The only way for us to stay out of the pit and not make it a way of life is to humble ourselves to the help and guidance of God's model for healing…we have to be *vulnerable and humble* and open up all our our heart to Him and His people to help us.

Here are three truths that will prevent many pit-trips and will also pull us out when we find ourselves there:

1- Accept the reality that we cannot heal on our own apart from God, His Word, and His people. This is the hardest truth for people to accept because people either want to try to "clean up" without God and then give Him a report, or just keep it between them and God and reject His people. Trying to clean up by ourself takes us down a dead-end every time. And then we forfeit the full manifestation of healing by refusing help from the people God wants to work through.

What this kind of thinking comes down to is "leaning *into* our own understanding" and it takes us back to the pit every time. Until we're willing to be humble, vulnerable, and accountable to a group of sound-minded people who are balanced in God's grace and truth, and show us empathy and understanding, we're always on our way back to the pit–period. But when we open up then we have an opportunity to reveal our real self...the flawed, shamed, and sinful parts of ourself that keeps using a counterfeit means to connect, because being real is too risky. (2 Cor 3:18; Phil 1:9-11; Col 1:10)

2- Take ownership and look into our hearts to begin the emotional work required to find out what unmet needs are driving our negative behaviors. When our real self that represents our personality has been judged, then our real self has to go into hiding. From it's hidden place in our heart, it begins to seek the acceptance it needs through a counterfeit means like rage, narcissism, eating disorders, substance abuse, rejecting weaknesses and badness, guilt, depression, sexual addiction, body dysphoria, perfectionism, etc. This list is extensive and it's where the majority of us have issues because we have not brought these parts of our heart into the light of God's love, grace, and healing with Him and His people.

To experience the healing that's available this side of Heaven as God promises, we have to be actively "working out our salvation" as Philippians 2:12 instructs. Work is an understatement; this isn't for the faint-hearted as one of my friends describes it. You will hear me say this over and over. There are no shortcuts and we *can't* dumb-down the hard work, but we *can* expect to move through and heal because it's God's promise! We can rely on His Holy Spirit to be our 24/7 Helper and Advocate. (John 14: 25-26, 16:5-15; Phil 2:12-13)

3- Put into practice steps one and two and keep doing these things over and over as a way of life. This is the critical component to us living a healthy and balanced life. When people return to a former lifestyle that's unhealthy or relapse into some kind of addictive behavior, one of the first things I do is retrace their steps to see patterns, and *patterns don't lie*! Patterns reveal the subtle direction change that happens in our heart and eventually manifests into visible behavior changes. Inevitably, a person will pull away from the people who love and speak truth to them; they will emotionally distance themselves, pull back, and turn away…especially from the people who are more perceptive and can pick up on "something different" that is going on.

Negative internal heart changes are not sudden, although it seems that way. The internal changes have been developing for years in the hidden part of their heart. Anytime our heart deviates from the basics of the love blueprint that God designed for us our life will manifest negative results. The key to staying on course is daily confession that involves, seeking God and asking Him to search our heart and connecting and opening up our heart with God's people who are grounded in His love, grace, and truth

Following Jesus is a way of life—a commitment to walk out the grace and truth that we have been given and then give it to others. This is the real Christian life...we can royally mess up and still be deeply loved! It's what God's grace looks like in action. And when we're loved like this, we can accept our less-than parts and integrate them with our loved parts to have the strength to heal and become whole—letting our real self be known. But we have to know that when we call out for help, we will be unconditionally loved and accepted. And this is what gives us the courage to move forward with hope! This is God's system for healing and it works. (James 5:16; Lk 5:31; 1 Cor 11:28, 31)

Our willpower isn't enough to keep us out of the pit —*but God's love is*. When we submit our will to His power...we have His willpower to heal. Our willpower motivates us to *start* the race, but it's God's love that *sustains* us to run, endure, and win the race! God's love is perfected in our weakness. Will you let God's love be perfected in your weakness and help pull you out of the pit? ❤LMM

8. Suck it up Buttercup…

"I sought the Lord, and he answered me;
he delivered me from all my fears. Those who look to
him are radiant; their faces are
never covered with shame."

Psalm 34:4-5 (NIV)

Were you ever told, "suck it up Buttercup" when you were feeling overwhelmed, disappointed, angry, or some other negative emotion about a situation? Many people grew up hearing this saying or something similar. The intent of the message is to enable a person to face reality and deal with it–to "suck it up Buttercup" and move on. But this kind of message doesn't enable, it disables. A person learns to deny what they are feeling and that disables their ability to discern God's truth. God put emotions in us; they play a vital role in our well-being. If we do not learn how to contain them in healthy ways, we will be like Buttercup and suck up and suck up until we implode or explode!

Denial always makes a bad situation worse. Here are just a few examples in Scripture where denial undermines our God-given responsibilities to:

• take ownership for what's in our heart–we can't own what we deny (Prov 4:23).

• connect with the Body of Christ–we can't connect if we deny having needs (Ecc 4:10).

• mourn with those who mourn–we can't grieve with others if we're denying the grief process (Rom 12:15).

• speak truth–we can't speak truth if we deny what we're feeling (Eph 4:15).

• embrace grace–we can't embrace grace if we rely on our self-sufficiency (Prov 3:34).

Here are three steps that will help us be more aware of when we deny our feelings, and the practical steps to begin to reverse the process:

1- Feelings are real. When we feel our feelings, we are dealing with reality; they initiate the action we need to take to address the issue we're facing. So if we are overwhelmed with life in some way, we need to seek God for wisdom, and godly counsel in the Body of Christ to talk through what we're facing.

Talking through our feelings doesn't promise a change in our situation, but it does validate how we "feel". And validation is our bridge to reality because we experience understanding from someone and we feel their love. This is the incarnational love of Jesus Christ being manifested through us, the Body of Christ. This is huge and it's why reaching out is so critical. If we deny our feelings, we lose touch with reality.

When you hear about supposedly sane people doing insane things…it's often people who have denied their feelings and those feelings took on a life of their own in their hearts. This insane behavior can be anything from illicit sex, embezzling money, drowning children, to homicide-suicide situations. There are numerous other horrific situations, but they all began with denying feelings in the heart, and denied feelings will implode or explode. (1 Ptr 4:9; Eph 4:25; 1 Thess 2:4)

2- Feelings are our built-in emotional dashboard; they are God's design for us to communicate and relate. For example, our first two years of life are pre-verbal; before we can process thoughts or communicate with words, we have to rely on our feelings to communicate what we need. As we grow and develop, our feelings are our means to connect and relate our desires, passions, concern, etc. Our feelings also signal us to respond or take action. Anxiety can alert us to danger, anger lets us know something has been violated, and sadness says we've lost something– you get the point, right? We are responsible for taking good care of our emotional dashboard because "it determines everything we do". (Prov 4:23; Eph 2:9; Gal 3:3)

3- *Feel* the feelings we've been denying, *process* the pain surrounding them and   *understand* how we've been impacted. Nothing changes overnight, but the relief that comes with "being heard" is ginormous! It is the incarnational love of Jesus Christ experienced in human flesh…and it's God's design. God tells us over and over throughout Scripture that He will never leave us. He pours His love through us to reach each other; we are the Body of Christ. He uses us as His vessels for each other to manifest the supernatural power of His grace. God's grace boggles our mind and heals our heart. We decide if we will open up our heart to the transforming power of grace. (Ecc 7:3; Luke 6:49; Rom 12:15)

If you've been following a Buttercup model for dealing with your feelings, I pray you will seek God's guidance. James 1:2 gives us clear instruction: "we are only fooling ourselves if we don't do what God's Word says." When we acknowledge what we're feeling and open up to trusting people who will listen without judgment we are at a place where change happens. Will you open your heart to the change God promises? ❤LMM

9. Failure is inevitable– not final

"There is a path before each person that seems right, but it ends in death."

Proverbs 14:12 (NLT)

We are going to experience failure–it's an inevitable reality that none of us can avoid, but it doesn't have to be a final chapter. However, by the the time people make an appointment with me to talk about their failure…

They. Feel. Like. A. Failure.

And what they are feeling is valid because they've experienced so much failure! Most people who are stuck in failure patterns aren't stuck for a lack of not trying on their part. They tried hard, but failure won: another affair, divorced again, estranged relationships, financial strain, career issues, ministry problems, missed opportunities, dead dreams, and on and on. Failure means we tried–but *if we do not learn anything about the patterns we used in our trying* we will just keep trying and failing with the same patterns that perpetuate failure. And it's when failure is perpetuated in marriages, families, careers, finances, and ministries, etc. that a person begins to lose hope.

Facing failure is hard work, but we're promised a good return on our investment when we face it the right way. The good news is we don't have to grope through the dark and hope we're going down the right path…we can be confident. Our confidence is found in God's Word. He gives us clear instruction on how we can face failure and overcome it. Failure is inevitable, not final. Our part is to face, embrace, and take ownership of failure so that we can learn from it. Here are three steps to get us moving in the right direction:

1- Reflect on the situation. We can't move on from a failure that we haven't faced. So the first thing we need to do when the reality of failure sinks in is to sit down with God and ask Him to search our heart for our part in the failure. To hear God, we need to give Him our undivided attention. This means we take time to give Him all of our mind, heart, spirit, and strength.

God corrects us to make us right, not wrong. God corrects those He loves–His correction reroutes us like a good GPS and gets us on the right path. But if a person has not learned to take responsibility for their failure or has been shamed, ridiculed, or punished harshly, they will resist the godly correction they need to turn around and go in the right direction. They hear godly correction as criticism.

When we have a failure we need to be cognizant of our tendency to talk to God while we're on our way to do something else. But when our Father, the Creator of the Universe, gives us an open-door policy to talk to Him anytime night or day and we pass on it because we are busy doing other things...go figure regarding the reasons failure dominates. We are privileged to have 24/7 access to our Father. He promises to listen and give guidance–it's during our hardest seasons that God does His greatest work in us...if we let Him. (Heb 12:6; Prov 3:11, 28:26; Rev 3:20)

2- Revise the plan. Many people try harder using the same negative patterns that led to their former failure. Of course, this always leads to another failure. *Instead of seeing their pattern of behavior as the problem, they see the situation or relationship as the problem* and they "throw in the towel". *For a person to break negative patterns, they must have an understanding of what's driving their patterns.* The answer is always found in our heart, where our patterns develop. When we take responsibility for what's in our heart—our desires, beliefs, and behaviors—then we have voice and a say in the outcome. This step is key to resolving failure patterns.

God knows we can't do this alone and He provides us help. Our part is to actively seek Him for the guidance in choosing wise counsel who will encourage us to stay on course, while equipping us with the experiences to replace the old negative patterns with healthy ones, and that can help us connect the dots in understanding what drives the patterns and our behaviors. Until our patterns are traced back to their origin in our heart, we will spend a lifetime managing patterns, instead of resolving them... and that is an exhausting prison of its own kind! (Prov 16:1, 16:9; Ecc 7:3-4)

3- Regain footing. I've had many clients who "sit themselves on the bench" for years after a big failure with the intent to grow up and mature. Their logic made sense, but removing ourselves from situations where we experienced failure doesn't resolve the issues that led to our failure...we just suspend the behavior until it's repeated again.

Time away without a plan is just time away; it doesn't translate into having "new relational skills". The solution for regaining footing is practice, practice, practice…healthy patterns with healthy people in safe friendships, mentoring relationships, process-based Bible groups, small groups, and Christian individual and group therapy.

Consistent practice in these settings reinforces the transformational power of God's grace in our heart. This is where we need to remember the power of grace. Grace is the power that raised Jesus from the dead! And it is the power that will begin to internally change our negative patterns of behavior and replace them with new, healthy patterns as we cooperate and practice with God's Holy Spirit, Who lives in our spirit. This process is always slower than we want it to be, but we can't rush the repairs to our foundation–they take time to set up. But we can anticipate that the internal change of healthy patterns that happens in our hearts will lead us to the stable living Jesus promises us in life! (Heb 5:14, 10:25; Prov 14:12, 15:22)

God does His greatest work in us during our hardest seasons…if we will let Him. Failure is inevitable–not final. Will you commit to reflecting on the situation, revising your plan, and regaining your footing God's way? ❤LMM

10. Making your mess into a message…

"But the lord stands beside me like a great warrior. Before him my persecutors will stumble. They cannot defeat me. They will fail and be thoroughly humiliated. Their dishonor will never be forgotten."

Jeremiah 20:11(NIV)

We could sort through our messes much quicker if we had a more realistic view of ourselves. Most of us are much more shocked about our messes than God is. I'm not minimizing either the magnitude of our messes or the pain they may have caused us or others. But what I am saying is that our messes are turned into messages when we release them into the hands of our Father. God is a good Father; He's waiting to help us get back on track, but He can't help what we won't release from our hands or hearts. Many *intellectually* know this truth in their head, but they have not *emotionally* moved through the process in their heart– and they are stuck.

This topic is near and dear to my heart because I was stuck for several years in my emotional messes –I kept trying to move forward but God kept taking me back to deal with them. Finally, I relented (surrendered) and after much work and heartache guided by His hand and His people I began working through them! My past emotional messes no longer hold me hostage to the threats of being exposed! When we release our messes into God's hands, *the things that once confined us become the things that now define us*! Our messes are transformed into messages for God's glory and our good. I pray you won't choose to stay stuck in your mess one more day because…you don't have to.

Here are three steps that will help you:

1- Embrace God's correction: God put a profound word on my heart years ago that changed my life: "*I correct you to make you right, not wrong.*" If we're open to correction, we can be fully used by God. We were created to do good works that He planned long ago and God is committed to correcting us into walking them out. God will sculpt, shape, press, squeeze, add on, take away, build us up and tear us down because He's forever committed to developing our character to walk out the purpose He put in us. Correction is not a punishment. Punishment looks *back* and says "pay up" for the wrongs you've done. Correction looks *forward* and says, "I want to make you right because I love you." Correction is a teaching tool—welcome it. (Heb 12:6; Prov 3:12; Rev 3:19)

2- Grieve the choices you made. Grief is our friend, even though it hurts. But it's a hurt that leads to an end and opens the door to God's hope. Until we take ownership of the choices we've made and the ones we wished we had or hadn't made—those parts of our heart are removed from the love, healing, and relationship they need and we will be consumed with shame, sorrow, resentment, bitterness, anxiety, anger, jealousy, fear, and on and on. And those parts of our heart will turn against us and condemn us. These parts also turn from the love and protection of God's grace and become the enemy's playground. We can't move on from what we won't face and grieve. (Rom 8:31, 12:3; 1 John 3:20-22)

3- Stay connected when we mess up. It's critical that we don't turn away from the love and grace that we need to turn around. Our natural tendency is to be physically present, but emotionally estranged; we go through the motions, but reject the grace we need to heal. Grace enables us to experience God's love coming directly from Him and directly through His people—it's the privilege we have as children of God. When we are in our worst, most despicable day and we are accepted without judgment and met with kind eyes and a loving smile saying, "I understand, I am for you, I'm standing beside you" then we have experienced the incarnational love of Jesus through the Body of Christ. (James 5:15; 1 Ptr 4;8; 1 John 3:18)

Will you open up your heart and accept the grace you need to move you out of your mess? ❤LMM

NOTES

Chapter Four

Implementing truth -
the action plan

*"Jesus said to the people who believed in him, "You
are truly my disciples if you remain faithful to my
teachings. And you will know the truth, and the truth
will set you free."*

John 8:31-31 (NLT)

Our fourth stage of development is implementing truth...the action plan. This is where the three previous stages culminate and launch us into adulthood. Most kids can't wait to grow up and become an adult. Most of us made the statement, or something similar, like: "I can't wait until I'm an adult so I can be the boss!" We had no idea how true our statement was or the charge of responsibilities that come with adulthood. God's design is for us to progressively move through our emotional stages of development successfully so that we are prepared to assume the authority that bears His image.

Entering into adulthood is often referred to as "adulting", to use a currently popular expression, because it requires us to face the full scope of life's demands. It's a ginormous change from the days of checking off the chore list to being responsible for overseeing it, from helping unload groceries to being responsible for buying them, from having a part-time job to cover the nonessentials to needing a full-time job for the essentials, from only focusing on our personal needs to focusing on and being responsible for the family's needs, and on and on.

These realities affirm...

Adulting. Is. Difficult.

I'm kind of joking, but I'm really not. The big problem with not having our emotional needs met before entering adulthood is...our *chronological* age qualifies us to take on the charge of responsibilities, but our *emotional* age disqualifies us from carrying them out. The gap in between the two results in a host of emotional and psychological issues that result in a person entering adulthood with an emotional limp. Their emotional limp robs them of the truth that sets them free because they do not have understanding and experiences in the basics of love that are to be internalized during the progressive emotional stages of development. There's no amount of talent, charisma, beauty, superior intelligence, connections, possessions or endless resources that can make up for or replace our unmet emotional needs. This reasoning promises a path that leads to a dead end.

This final chapter can be a bit daunting regarding the "issue list", so before you read these, ask the Holy Spirit to help you hear what He wants you to hear. The unmet emotional needs from previous stages will obviously linger in this stage, like feelings of not belonging, poor boundaries, and an inability to reconcile good and bad, but these are usually overshadowed by authority issues, from rebelling to over compliance, breaking all the rules to rigidly following rules, constantly challenging every rule to doing everything without question, inferiority or superiority, romanticizing the younger years of childhood, sexual acting out or dysfunction, passive-aggressive, judgmental, inhibited, sexual dysfunction, depression, and fear of failure.

To make our life work...we need to seek the One Who created us and spoke this world into existence. He promises us freedom when we embrace His ways and He promises to send us the help we need. The following 10 situations are the boundary situations that I most see in my practice, and that people are most prone to get stuck in, how the unmet needs manifest when they go untreated, the symptoms that most people experience, and the three-part practical application to getting on the road to recovery. I pray you will receive the encouragement the Holy Spirt will give you as you move forward, knowing with confidence that He is your Helper and Healer! ❤LMM

1. Consider troubles an opportunity for great joy–
what???

*"Dear brothers and sisters, when troubles come your
way, consider it an opportunity for great joy."*

James 1:2 (NLT)

If I wasn't a Christian, I would consider this
Scripture to be a bad joke…the language seems to
oppose the basic emotional need for security that
God Himself put in our heart. But the verse is clear:
when troubles come our way, consider them an
opportunity for great joy. Are you kidding me???
We know God's not kidding us…but what does this
truth look like in our life?

In the years that I've counseled and coached
people, many know this verse to be true in their
spirit, but most have trouble processing it in their
minds, working through it in their hearts, and then
walking it out in their lives. The verse seems to
oppose the need for safety that God put in our
hearts, but it's actually the verse that will transform
our lives if we embrace it in the biblical way God
intends for us!

I've witnessed and lived the manifestation of God's
promise in this verse in my life, and in the lives of
my family, friends, and clients. James 1:4 confirms
the transformation, "so that you may be mature and
complete, not lacking anything." I used to read this
verse and think, "how can we not lack anything"?
But I have revelation of this verse now– not lacking
anything is our ongoing character development
that is *submitted* to Christ, *shaped* in trials, and

walked out in our reality to meet the inevitable demands of life!

Here are the three steps I personally and professionally rely on to keep me anchored in God's hope during trials:

1- To welcome a trial *doesn't mean we act happy about something that makes us sad*. When we welcome a trial we acknowledge God's sovereignty in our reality—He holds it all together in His hands. The despair, hopelessness, fear, etc. that our hearts feel is real; God doesn't expect us to not feel it. He wants us to call out to Him for help. God hears His people when we call out to Him and He rescues us from all our troubles! (Col 1:17; Ps 34:4, 17-19)

2- We know trials are a reality of life, but if we don't know how to move through our reality...trials will keep us stuck in life. But we are never left to the mercy of a trial. God promises to give us wisdom generously without finding fault. We have to decide if we will rely on His wisdom or human wisdom. We do not have to settle for staying stuck, but for us to keep a *sane mind and strong heart* while going through, our faith must be in His power and not human wisdom. We have to seek the One Who reigns over all we see and don't see. (1 Cor 2:5; James 1:5; Phil 4:7)

3- When a trial hits, God will do one of two things: stop it or move us through it. He is more likely to move us through it. Moving us through is what builds up our faith. Until we embrace this reality, we place ourselves on standby for our desired outcomes. Our standby unknowingly rejects the help God sends for us to move through the trial because we wait for our desired outcome of the trial instead of trusting God to empower us to move through it. (Ps 9:10, 145:9; Phil 2:12-13)

God will make a way when we can't…will you let Him? ❤LMM

2. The "middle part" of believing…

"When you pass through the waters, I will be with you; and when you pass through the rivers, they will not sweep over you. When you walk through the fire, you will not be burned; the flames will not set you ablaze."

Isaiah 43:2 (NIV)

When God put the word, "the middle part of believing" on my heart years ago, I had no idea how it would profoundly change my life. The "middle part of believing" is *leaving what we know, while on the way to what we don't know*. Most of us don't leave our familiar because we chose to…we leave because we didn't have a say, we had no place to stay, the season ended, we were not invited back, were pushed out, replaced, or circumstances changed that we had no control over. Can you relate to any of these?

- home foreclosures
- evictions
- church leadership changes
- we regret to inform you that _____
- uninvited from family, friends, or groups
- death
- medical report
- breakups
- affairs
- divorces
- companies downsizing

This isn't an exhaustive list, but you get the picture. We don't choose these kind of things…they are placed on us. These things catapult us into the "middle part" of believing. The middle is an uncomfortable, uncertain, and unfamiliar place– it exposes insecurities, purges pride, and tests what we profess to believe. I questioned God's intentions: "What am I doing wrong"? "Why is this taking so long"? Finally relief came, but it wasn't because God had answered me or that I had reached the other side…it was because I had finally embraced were I was. I no longer *wished* I could be in the former familiar that was behind me. I no longer wanted to "hurry up" and be where I was going. I no longer "wanted more" from the moment I was in to be okay. I let go of the conditions I had on "being okay". This letting go was my surrender to live in now, to live in the "middle part" of believing while looking ahead to the other side.

Whether God places us in the middle, a person's harm puts us there, or an unfortunate situation lands us there– when we're there we come to know the love of God deeper than ever before! We're certain He's with us, we know His voice, He knows our name, and will never leave us. God will use the circumstances for His glory and our good, but we must let go and let Him lead the way. Here are three steps that will get us embracing the "middle part of believing":

1- Embrace the trial…sounds so crazy, but it's God's way that transforms us into His image. God never expects us to clap and smile about the trials– that would be fake. But we can humbly ask Him for wisdom to empower us with His grace to have the stamina we need to keep moving and doing what He asks of us…and He will answer our request! (James 1:5; Phil 2:13; 2 Cor 3:18)

2- Take ownership of how we feel, what's in our heart, and the things that were lost or taken without our input or consent. This is the place where we weep, get mad, consider giving up, question hearing God's direction, feel sorry for ourselves, and ask God through fits and tears what He wants from us, *and it's where He does His greatest work in us*–Hallelujah! (Prov 4:23; Gal 6:9; Isa 40:31)

3- God always sends us help–He is faithful and always sends a word of encouragement and an understanding friend to help us stay on course....especially during our weariest moments. When we arrive to the other side, we're ready not because we're there, we're ready because we are known by God's love and we know His voice. We know without a doubt that we can trust Him and that He will never leave us, always keep His promises, and is undeniably the source for all our needs. (Isa 43:2; Prov 6:22; Ps 73:24)

Whether God places us in the middle, a person's harm puts us there, or an unfortunate situation lands us there– we come to know the love of God deeper than ever before! We're certain He's with us and will never leave us. Are you embracing your "middle part of believing"? ❤LMM

3. The wrenching decisions we must make…

*"If any of you lacks wisdom, you should ask God,
who gives generously to all without finding fault,
and it will be given to you."*

James 1:5 (NIV)

If you've ever experienced the wrenching heartache that comes with releasing a situation to God and then trusting Him to provide…you know first-hand the nearly inconsolable pain I'm talking about– especially if it's a loved one. These kinds of decisions can make a person cry non-stop for days! These decisions are part of the reality of living and walking out the faith that we profess to believe, and there's nothing easy about it! But when we know we're doing what God's called us to do and that the pain is making a difference, it empowers us to follow through. But even when we know that we are making the right decision, it can still feel so wrong because…it hurts so bad!

I'm certain in hindsight that my hard decisions were the cooperation and catalyst God needed to open the door of provision in my situations. But in my grief, I began to second-guess my decisions. One time in particular I heard the confident whisper of God's truth in my spirit say, "authentic love prefers the needs of the other, even when it feels like it's killing both of you." This clear word confirmed my decision, but it didn't take away the hurt in my heart. My hurt had to run it's course; it's the good hurt that roots us deeper in God's love, grows our faith in His hope during trials, and puts *His truth, instead of our truth*, on the throne of our heart. For us to make this kind of hurt be purposed, we have to rely on God's wisdom, and here are three steps to start us in that direction:

1- Cooperation is the catalyst. Our cooperation is the catalyst God needs to open the door of provision to impossible situations we face, but still the grief that comes with releasing a loved one or situation where there is so much potential loss at stake is almost unbearable because it creates an onslaught of second-guessing. It's in these vulnerable and broken moments when the enemy will question us from a human perspective about our Spirit-led decisions. "Spirit-led" is the operative phrase and anchor of hope that we can cling to in these heartbreaking times. Our human mind cannot discern matters that are Spirit-led revelation, nor are we supposed to. Our part is to submit to the Holy Spirit's lead. We submit because we trust Him, even when we don't understand what He's doing.

This desire to obey and follow through protects us. If we do not have insight regarding this truth, we will fall prey to the enemy's mind-games because he challenges us from our human understanding. But we don't need to understand these difficult decisions when we trust the Holy Spirit's lead—boom! And this protects us because God opposes the proud, the enemy, and gives grace to the humble—that's us. (Prov 28:26; 1 Cor 2:13; James 4:6)

2- Doing what's right doesn't negate pain. As reassuring as God's voice is in our spirit, it doesn't take away the hurt in our heart. And this is where we have to be careful and not confuse our pain of grief as a sign that we're not doing the right thing. Grief has to run it's course; it roots us deeper in God's love, grows our faith in His hope, and enables His authentic truth to reign in our heart instead of us preferring our truth...but it's still some of the hardest work we will ever do! (2 Cor 12:9-10; James 1:2-6)

3- Response determines disposition. How we respond to God's wisdom determines the disposition of our heart: we will either resort to human solutions by shutting the door to His provisions or we will rely on Him to open the door. *There's no human solution for impossible situations, but God's sufficiency promises to make a way.* Turning to God enables His power to be perfected in our weaknesses. And when we do the right thing and trust His wisdom, we partner with Him and experience His promises in our life. (1 Cor 2:5; Eph 3:16; Phil 4:13)

Are you facing a situation where you need to do the right thing, but the thought of carrying it out seems inconceivable? God's for you...will you trust Him to walk you through this situation? ❤LMM

4. Embracing the places we don't want to be...

"Let perseverance finish its work so that you may be mature and complete, not lacking anything. If any of you lacks wisdom, you should ask God, who gives generously to all without finding fault, and it will be given to you."

James 1:4-5 (NIV)

Embracing the places we don't want to be is where God will do His greatest work in us– it's where our character is developed. Our character development is crucial in walking out the plans of God. A person who has the greatest talent and access to unlimited resources will fail miserably apart from character development. Character catapults us forward and enables us to face the demands of life and carry out the cause God put in our heart. But the disclaimer is: the emotional growing pains that accompany character development are excruciating because we're often the innocent victim in bad situations. And the insult to injury is that usually it's in the situations where we are being obedient and following God. Does this scenario sound familiar? Here's a hint in Luke 22:42: "Father, if you are willing, please take this cup of suffering away from me. Yet I want your will to be done, not mine."

Jesus is the model for embracing the places we *don't want to be*...so that God can develop us for the places He *needs us to be* and the character we need to demonstrate there. The Gospels are full of examples of Jesus modeling the character development we need in adulthood:

• actions motivated by love instead of fear

- said "no" when He needed to
- admitted what was in His Heart
- stood up to bullying religious leaders
- asked for emotional support from close friends
- walked in the authority God gave Him
- didn't try to prove Himself
- loved when others were not loving
- forgave unconditionally
- set limits on evil
- gave grace and spoke truth
- carried His Cross until the end despite the dismal and hopeless-looking situation in front of Him, to fulfill the purpose His Father put in Him!

There are certainly more examples, but this list represents the character we need in adulthood every day to make life work. Any area of character in which we are undeveloped will manifest into an emotional deficit that's acted out in a negative behavior. These behaviors are polar opposites—a person will experience one side of the extreme behavior like: superior or inferior, controlling or passive, rebellious or overly compliant, argumentative or overly agreeable, one up or one down, idealize or undermine authority, dependent or isolated, too serious or not serious enough, etc. Until we take ownership for these kinds of behavior, *we will walk with an emotional limp in life*.

Here are three truths to help us begin to take ownership:

1- God never promised us *fair*...He promises us *power*! A life committed to Christ doesn't exempt us from hardships and heartaches, but God promises He will never leave us and that He will supernaturally make a way when it's humanly impossible. Our willingness to embrace unfair situations gives God the opportunity to develop our character. We acknowledge the harm intended towards us, but we rely on the power of God's grace flowing through us and from His people who are standing with us to be gracious and kind to those who harmed us. I have experienced the incredible grace of God and it has enabled me to walk in freedom. I pray you won't pass on this freedom. (Ps 34:18; Luke 18:27; Isa 45:2)

2- Ask the Holy Spirit what He wants to teach you in these difficult places. God put this Word in my Spirit years ago and it has changed the trajectory of my life—it will change yours, too! Our tendency is to ask God "why" He's doing or letting (fill in the blank). There's nothing wrong with questioning, but if we get stuck on "why" then we will miss "what" He wants us to teach us in these places. But if we opt out, we forfeit the character work and strengthening He will do in us. Character is the key to having the "spiritual mojo" to move through all the inevitable unfair situations we will face. (Phil 4:19; Gen 50:20; Eph 3:20)

3-Faith doesn't grow unless it's tested. When we go into unknown places and face uncomfortable situations, we will experience a desperation that drives us to the reality that we need a Savior every second until we see Him face-to-face. This positions us to remain humble, which enables us to remain strong and to succeed in impossible situations— because God's power is perfected in our weaknesses. (2 Cor 12:9; Ps 66:10, 92:12)

Embracing the places *we don't want to be is the only way for God to develop the character in us for the places He needs us to be.* These places are opportunities, so welcome the growth God will do in and through you–it's the kind of transformation that no devil in hell will ever be able to steal! The next time you're in a place you don't want to be will you ask the Holy Spirit what He wants to teach you there? ❤LMM

5. Hands up on Sunday– laid out on Monday!

*"The thief's purpose is to steal and kill and destroy.
My purpose is to give them a rich and satisfying life."*

John 10:10 (NLT)

 Do you remember the last time you had your hands up and praising Jesus on Sunday? The struggle you carried into worship was beating you down– but after worship you were refreshed and ready to face things. Then Monday morning came and the overwhelming struggle returned with a vengeance! This is what I call, "Hands up on Sunday...laid out on Monday". In Sunday worship our problems had no power, but on Monday morning–they flooded us with discouragement. All of us have had this happen at times, but it's when it happens most Mondays that's when we have a pattern that points to a problem.

 This situation is more common than we think. I see it in my practice all the time–we just don't talk about it as much as we need to. None of us are exempt from this, but the people I'm talking about who get stuck on Monday mornings...are Jesus- loving, praying hard, professing God's Word, giving their time to godly causes kind of people. But they also seem to have a cloud of chaos following them everywhere. We know the Christian life doesn't exempt us from facing many trials and sorrows, Jesus clearly tells us this in John 16:33. He's also clear in John 10:10 that the thief comes to steal, kill, and destroy, but He's come to give us a rich and satisfying life. So what's the pattern that points to the problem??? It's not their worship–this person loves Jesus...their hands are up and loving on Jesus every time they're in worship. It's not their praying, professing, or giving of their time—they are actively involved in these areas. It's what they're not doing that's creates a pattern that points to their problem.

When I meet with people who experience this and they tell me about this chaotic cloud, I explain their situation has a lot of logical explanations that can be fixed with very practical applications. The cloud of chaos represents a state of being, confusion, and disorder— it's the status quo for their life. Chaos differs from the seasons of sorrow and trials or even most of the enemy's attacks that Jesus tells us about in John. We default to living a chaotic life when we are not actively participating in our character growth with God and His people. We can be the most gifted and talented person in the world with access to an unlimited amount of financial resources, but all this is a bust if we are not actively seeking God first, and then His people, to get help with the growth and development of our character. James 1:2-4 spells it out: "Consider it pure joy, my brothers and sisters, whenever you face trials of many kinds, because you know that the testing of your faith produces perseverance. Let perseverance finish its work so that you may be mature and complete, not lacking anything."

This is why God brings us through more trials than He takes away or takes us around. Character is rooted in His love beginning in our early development; it enables us to face and move through the demands of life and "not lack anything". Character keeps on doing the right thing when others aren't, when we don't feel like it, and when it seems to make no difference...but we know that we will reap a harvest—*if we don't quit*!

To stop the chaos cloud from overshadowing our life, we will need to embrace these three biblical truths to begin to turn around:

1- Our first step is to always go to God first and humbly ask for His wisdom. He will give it generously without finding fault and show us the character issues that are disabling us emotionally. (Ps 139:4, 139:23-24; James 1:5; Gal 6:9)

2- God promises to transform us, but our transformation requires our participation. We profess His Word and actively participate in the process by taking ownership of the the things in our heart that oppose God's truth, shine a light on the struggles that continue to cause us problems, speak truth, take responsibility for those we've caused harm to, stop debating God's truth, and ask Him to help us to embrace it. This is the daily grind of working out our salvation, but the grind pays a great dividend. (Heb 10:35-36; Phil 1:6, 2:12-13; Eph 4:14-15)

3- Accepting help from God and the help He sends through His people. Over and over I see the hand of God send people help, but their pride rejects the help; they want to do it their way and go it alone— and this response to help promises that the cloud of chaos will continue to follow them. We learned our unhealthy character patterns of behavior in unhealthy relationships. To unlearn them, we need healthy, godly people who can teach and give us the experience we need to practice these patterns of relating. We need *both* God's help *and* help from His people—i t's God's design. (Prov 14:9, 4:1212; Matt 7:8; Rom15:14).

I pray you will keep your hands up praising God on Sundays, but will you also humbly seek help so that you're not continually laid out on your back on Monday. Will you commit to participate in the character process? ❤LMM

6. The Counseling Toolbox

"For my words are wise, and my thoughts are filled with insight."

Psalm 49:3 (NLT)

Do you remember the last time you were in a situation where you felt emotionally side-swiped or overwhelmed with feelings that made you feel out of control? Maybe you had an argument with a family member. It could of been a work issue where you were criticized. Possibly you're in a relationship now where you continue to "lose it". There are several more examples, but you get the gist of what I'm saying. We experience different emotions for different reasons in different situations, but the answer to resolving our different emotions is always the same…we need to be heard, understood, and have help. God designed it this way for us to connect and communicate in a safe setting so that we can make the changes we need to fulfill the purpose He put in us. Until we experience His design for us, we will forever be in some kind of emotional vortex and exhausted with life.

All of us have been in the kind of situations mentioned above, but not all of us are in touch with our emotions when we are. Some people have been taught to minimize and deny what they are feeling. Others learned long ago to hide their emotions in an attempt to protect themselves. And then others believe having demonstrative feelings is weak and immature. I've heard a zillion views over the years in counseling sessions, but I always have the same response…God gave us emotions and we need to know how to use them so that they work *for us instead of against us*.

For us to better understand our emotions, we need to first have a basic understanding of God's progressive order of our development. Our emotional development is primary–it's the foundation for cognition and language to root into the foundation of love. Cognition and language are a secondary development.

This is God's design and it's logical–we need to be loved and feel safe before we can think and develop language skills. Stable thoughts are rooted in a secure emotional foundation– unstable thoughts are rooted in an insecure emotional foundation. And it's this very reason that we can't "think or speak" our way out of being anxious, depressed, jealous, mad, sad, bitter, and so on–until someone meets us in our pain and helps us process what's going on in our head and heart. Although some people are able to "think and speak" themselves out of negative emotions for a period of time, it doesn't last because it undermines God's plans for us to resolve our heart issues. (Prov 4:23)

To help the people I counsel and coach, I write this concept on my whiteboard in sessions and workshops. I call it the "Counseling Toolbox"–the three tools every person needs to think clearly. These three tools are an integral part of our healthy emotional development. When used together and in order, they enable us to process our emotions and think about them so that we can manage our emotions...instead of them managing us.

1- Soothe feelings is our first tool. When we're overwhelmed with emotions and someone shows us compassion and concern, we are soothed. Soothing meets us in our pain and puts all our fragmented emotional parts back together again. As we experience soothing, we feel God's love directly from Him and through His people to calm us down. Over time we internalize this process and learn how to soothe ourselves, but the process never replaces the human connections we need. People who resist their feelings will struggle with a myriad of insecure thoughts because we have to be emotionally secure to have stable thoughts. (Phil 4:7; Col 3:15; Prov 20:5)

2- Validate experience is our next tool. When we're validated, we are understood and listened to—someone comes to us, stands with us, and sees from our perspective. It's what Jesus did in the Gospels:He went to the people—and they experienced His understanding. Validation enables us to experience another person being for us—it's the fuel that enables us to "stand back up". Validation is God's design. That design allows us to experience Him as the incarnate Body of Christ Who is always with us. (Phil 4:9; Eph 3:19; Isa 41:10)

3- Structured thinking, the tool that brings all the parts together. After we've been soothed and validated, we become calm and connected and have an emotional place to "root into". We have to be taught how to think about our emotions so that we can structure them. Emotions apart from structured thinking are a never-ending vortex. Structured thinking connects our thoughts and feelings so we can organize, prioritize, and be introspective. (Isa 26:3; Jer 17:7; Prov 20:5)

Will you ask God for wisdom to help you incorporate these three tools so that you can manage your emotions...*instead of them managing you*? ❤LMM

7. It's just the way I am...

"Give me understanding and I will obey your instructions; I will put them into practice with all my heart."

Psalm 119:34 (NLT)

Have you ever been in a heated exchange with someone you love and you told them if they really wanted to change they could? And their response to you was...

It's. Just. The. Way. I. Am.

Their response is correct, but their belief that they can't change is incorrect. Our patterns do accurately represent who we are...they are a culmination of everything we've learned in our life and are deeply ingrained into the structure of our personality. This is God's design. He prewired us to model behavior and then internalize it to make it our own so we could carry it forward to the next generation. If you didn't have good role models, don't worry—God has that part worked out; I'll explain in a bit.

I always share a funny story about my girls, when they were toddlers, to illustrate the influence we have on our children in areas we least expect. We were at the mall and walked up to a purse rack. We hadn't been there but a few seconds, when I noticed my three-year-old, Meg, had picked up a big purse and pressed her nose into it; immediately following her, was my two-year-old, Morgan, who did the same thing. It didn't occur to me at first what they were doing, then I realized...they were modeling my behavior! I would "sniff" a purse to determine if it was leather or pleather. I never instructed them to sniff a purse–they "sniffed" because I "sniffed". They observed my behavior and internalized it to make it their behavior. But they didn't know why they "sniffed"...they just knew that's what we did when we were around a rack of purses. And this is how we *observe, internalize, and put into practice* what we learn in our early relationships– even something as seemingly insignificant as "sniffing" a purse. There are three important takeaways about modeling behavior:

1. No formal instruction is required–only observation.

2. No explanation is needed–behavior witnessed is accepted as "the way".

3. No ability to discern between positive or negative behavior.

Based on the the takeaways above, it's easy to understand that a child is going to model what they see– they don't have the ability to discern negative and positive behavior in their role model. As you're reading this you might be recalling some negative role modeling that you internalized into your personality structure. If so, will you just take a minute and ask the Holy Spirit to shield your mind, heart, and spirit to any condemnation the enemy wants to try and unload on you?

It would be impossible to change our patterns of relating since they are so deeply ingrained into our personality structure, but we have the power and the promise of the Holy Spirit to show us the way. Just remember though, because it's *possible*...

doesn't mean it's easy. This is hard work, but it's worth it! Be on guard to the lies of the enemy; he doesn't want you to believe you can change these patterns...but he's a liar!!! So let's do this–here are three truths you need to know to begin to make the changes God promises:

1- Repeat patterns. We will repeat the negative patterns we despise because the emotional pattern is carved into the rules of our heart, which is hardwired to thought patterns in our brain. This is what makes people feel a little "crazy" because they are "compelled" to repeat patterns that cause pain in their life. An example would be someone who is drawn to "emotionally unavailable" people; the more "unavailable" the "unavailable" person is, the more intensity there is to pursue and try to please that person.

The desire to connect dismisses the evident rejection because the goal is to connect at all cost. And it often costs them a lot. This pattern of relating typically points back to a parent who was not emotionally available and possibly hostile in some ways. The pattern was set up in the child to "appease" this parent. The more the parent pushed *away*, the more the child pushed *in* to "win" the parent's love...and ever so often a connection would be made to reinforce the repetitive pattern. This is also similar to the negative repetitive pattern in a gambling addiction. No amount of convincing people of all the reasons they shouldn't be involved in these kind of relationships is going to work. Until this hardwiring is "rewired" this person will relate in this way. This often involves some therapy, but it's well worth the time and money compared to the future heartache and expense. (Mark 7:8; Matt. 15:3; Prov 2:10)

2- Reference point of familiar. We like familiar, even when it hurts and is uncomfortable. Sounds crazy, but it's true. Familiar gives us a sense of control, it's predictable, and we like to know what's going to happen next. But we don't consciously think these thoughts, they are deeply ingrained into our personality structure. We intuitively navigate to the familiar we know without thinking about it, and without realizing it…it perpetuates the pain we're trying to avoid. I see this a lot with people who can't keep a job. They are bright, talented, and likable people until their negative pattern of relating is pushed and then they explode on people. Companies will send this person to anger management classes and all the person learns is how to manage their anger for awhile until they "lose it".

Over the years, this person is kept on staff because the company has benefited from their talent and sees their potential "if they could work through" their anger issues. But eventually, the anger is more noticeable than the progress and the company has to let this person go. The dynamic that often takes place, is this person will be confronted with reasonable questions from others or their ideas will be challenged, but not in an oppositional way. However, the person with the anger issues will default to a pattern of behavior that is defensive, rude, and completely unprofessional. This person can often catch themselves at the onset of their pattern, but their need to feel in control is more important. Then they continue to the point of no return.

Usually the dynamic in this scenario is related to an inability to accept or tolerate any kind of negative input because either they were shamed in some way while growing up or the family was't allowed to speak about negative things...everybody had to be in a "happy-clappy Jesus" mood. The irony is the anger was never dealt with and is the default defense pattern that is wrecking this person's life. Until the connection is made to what's driving the behavior and integration in their heart happens, they will not be able to "accept" any kind of constructive input and will not be employable. (Prov 22:24; Gal 6:4-5; 1 Ptr 5:8)

3. Repairing the patterns: We learn our patterns during our formative years and they become engrained into our personality structure—our patterns will either make us or break us. To change we need God, His people, and new patterns of relating. If one part of this is missing...change will not happen. But when we admit we can't make the changes apart from God, are humble and ask for help from the Body of Christ, repent of our negative patterns of relating, continue to be actively involved in the learning process, be purposed in connecting to a grace- and truth-balanced people, continue to bring all the parts of our heart into relationship to be accepted and loved, give of our time and treasures, and obey God to the best we can—then we will consistently see a transformation and our negative patterns will be replaced with godly ones! (Zech 9:12; James 5:13-16; 1 Thess 1:7)

If we're breathing...we will have some kind of issue to work on until the day we see Jesus face-to-face. None of us escape brokenness, and each one of us has an opportunity to be healed. I pray you won't forfeit your opportunity. ❤LMM

8. I get what I'm doing...now what???

"Keep putting into practice all you learned and received from me--everything you heard from me and saw me doing. Then the God of peace will be with you."

Philippians 4:9 (NLT)

The coping skills we used to protect us as a child are the same skills that disconnect us as an adult. Unresolved hurt from childhood doesn't go away when we grow up, it just manifests into negative coping skills that disconnect us from the love we need to turn around. Unresolved hurt is insidious...it points a finger at the people who love us now and holds them hostage for the hurt we experienced back when we were a child. We will repeat our unhealthy coping skills from childhood like accusing, avoiding, blaming, complying, criticizing, complaining, controlling, embellishing, justifying, provoking, manipulating, etc. until we take ownership and work through our hurt. To do this we need God, His people, and all of our head, heart, spirit, and strength to open up and be available for relationship.

When we get to a place where we recognize a negative coping skill when it's happening– we have opened the door to a solution! Our unresolved issues manifest when we face conflict in relationships. Many people minimize, recoil, or leave when this happens and miss the work God will do through them in order to resolve the issue. If we will *embrace grace and hold tight to the truth*, God will empower us to work through the things we once hid from. Until we're willing to trust God to work through these relationship issues, we will cheat ourselves out of the deep connections we're promised. We have to keep our heart open to God and accountable to the Body of Christ as we continue to work through them.

But this is also where the hard work begins because the vulnerability we experienced as children that led us to being hurt…is the same vulnerability that's needed to connect and heal now as adults. The difference is, this time we will be in healthy and safe relationships so that we can heal. However, there will still be resistance, because our *emotional response* to being exposed will override our *intellectual understanding* and desire to be exposed. I don't want the reality of what to expect to overwhelm you, but I'm trying to prepare you so that you don't feel sideswiped. The most important thing to remember is

God. Will. Make. A. Way.

He wants us to heal emotionally and He will supernaturally empower us to face our hurt, open our heart to His people, and work through the things we once hid from. Will you let Him? If so, here are three of His truths that we must embrace to experience the healing He promises:

1- Recognize: we have to recognize our negative coping skills before we can face and overcome them. Our tendency is to pull away when we get hurt, but we must learn to push into the love we need to heal and move through the hurt. This feels beyond awkward and pretty scary because it involves dismantling the very coping skills we used to protect ourselves as a child when we felt vulnerable. Our internal emotional alarms will sound off and tell us to...shut down, hold back, and turn away, in an attempt to protect ourself from being vulnerable.

We didn't have a say as a child, but we have a say now. God promises to heal our hurt when we submit to His love, His truth, and His people. Then we get the love we didn't get as a child and learn the healthy coping skills we need now. Instead of pulling away when we get hurt, we learn to push into the love we need to overcome and move through the hurt. This is God's design and it works; our part is to internalize the love we're given. We are the manifolds of God's grace...we pour into each other and heal with the grace God's poured into us! (Lk 12:12; Ps 119:34; Prov 3:6)

2- Opening up: the next step is opening up our heart to internalize the love we're pushing into...the next level of awkwardness. And this is where a lot of people stop moving forward because it is emotionally excruciating to be this exposed. But it's this very exposure that enables the deep connections to take root. Have realistic expectations that you're going to have great success *and* fail miserably...none of us are exempt from this reality when internal heart changes are happening. If someone tells you that you should be moving at a faster speed or that they were able to move through with a step1, 2, 3, success—don't listen to one more word from them because they're not telling you the truth! We can understand in our head what we need to do, but struggle with carrying things out in our heart because it is hard work! (2 Chron 15:7; Deut 29:9; Ecc 4:9-12)

3- Keep on...keeping on. Our unresolved issues manifest when we face conflict in relationships, and our tendency is to check out, deny or leave when this happens and miss the work God will do through them. If we will embrace grace and hold tight to the truth, God will empower us to work through the things we once hid from. Until we're willing to trust God to work through these relationship issues, we will cheat ourselves out of the deep connections we're promised. We have to keep our heart open to God and accountable to the Body of Christ as we continue to work through them. But as we continue to respond, reach out, and rely on healthy relationships who love us with God's grace and acceptance...we "internalize these experiences" into our heart.

These internalized experiences of love and acceptance begin to fill the empty, hurting, anxious, afraid, shamed, condemned, and hopeless places in our heart. This is the power of God's transforming grace literally pouring into our heart and bringing together the fragmented, broken, and hidden pieces. The hard part is to consistently reach out and let people in on days when we're feeling bad about who we are. It's on these days when we are most vulnerable to the enemy whispering his lies: "we are a burden, we should be further down the road, etc. ". But it's these days that are the game-changers, because when we turn towards the healthy love we need...we experience that we are loved on our worst days! (James 1:22; Josh 1:6-7; John 1:12)

Our best isn't enough—if it was...we wouldn't need a Savior to save us. We cannot change with our will-power, but when we submit our will to God's power...He will empower us to change. Will you humbly submit yourself to the Lord so He will raise you up in due time? ❤LMM

9. Everything made beautiful in time...

"He has made everything beautiful in its time. He has also set eternity in the human heart; yet no one can fathom what God has done from beginning to end. "

Ecclesiastes 3:11 (NIV)

How are we supposed to have hope when our heart is breaking, our thoughts won't stop racing, and our family is failing at life??? When life's tragedies push us past our human threshold to deal with pain...there are no words in the human language to convey the grief we feel in our heart other than inaudible groans and wails. The scenes surrounding the situation are stuck in our head on replay and in slow motion— they seem so surreal, but our breaking heart confirms that they *are* real. How are we supposed to reconcile the hopelessness we feel with the faith we profess to believe???

When you have no hope
...praise Him

When your head is spinning out of control
...praise Him

When your heart is exploding into a million pieces
...praise Him

When it all seems surreal—but it's real
...praise Him

When you're drowning in despair
...praise Him

When only groans come from deep within you

...praise Him
When the ache in your heart won't stop
...praise Him

When there's no human solution to your situation
...praise Him

Life will push us past our human threshold to deal with pain, but never, ever past the power of God's love that lives in us. Here are three truths saturated with God's Word to remind you of the power of His love that lives in you:

1- God's timing is perfect; this is a truth—life is imperfect, this is a reality. His truth sometimes seems to contradict the hope and good plans He promises us. But our mind and heart can't comprehend the depth of His hope and His appointed time to bring things to pass and make them beautiful. Every time we do, *we take a ride on the highway to hell*. The sooner we can get to a place of putting our hope in God...the sooner He can give us the rest we need. (Ecc 3:11, 7:13, 8:17)

2- God's grief is the antidote to give us hope and heal our broken hearts. He does this through His people, you and me; we are God's people...He loves us through each other. We feel His love when we love each other, especially when we "mourn with those who mourn". God's people hold us up so that we can hold on; we can't grieve the love we lost... unless we have love to hold onto.

Despair consumes the heart of the person who has no one to hold onto. That's why Scripture says, "blessed are those who mourn, they will be comforted". As grief moves through us, it pushes us forward to the hope we are promised. Grief gets us through the pain, but it doesn't have us forget about the person. So many people are stuck in grief due to fear of forgetting their loved one. God understands this and He makes a way for us to reconcile our love and memory of the person we lost in our heart...while moving through the pain about them in our life. (Rom 12:14; Mt 5:4; Isa 43:18-19)

3- God's plan makes a way...even when we don't understand. Be careful to not let the evaluation of "why" take your focus off the revelation of "Who" is with you during trials. God promises hope in the middle of hopeless despair, when we put our hope in Him. His hope is an anchor for our soul; His hope holds on when ours is gone. His eyes are on those who love Him; He promises a peace that surpasses understanding. He's close to the brokenhearted and saves those who are crushed in spirit! There are so many things we will never understand this side of Heaven. To move forward requires us to put our hope in God...He makes everything beautiful in its time! (Ecc 7:3; Mt 5:14; Rom 12:15)

We can spend a lifetime trying to reconcile wrongs, unravel mysteries, and make sense of senseless situations and lose our mind along the way, *or we can choose to put our hope in God's love*. God is love and His love is full of power. He was before anything came to be, reigns over all we see and don't see, and holds it all together in His hands. His love heals every wrong ever done, soothes every moan in our soul, and makes everything beautiful in its time! Holy, Holy, Holy, Lord God Almighty, Maker of Heaven and Earth...will you commit to putting your hope in the One Who loved you first? ❤LMM

10. Enjoying Life 101...

"Finally, now, dear brothers and sisters, one final thing. Fix your thoughts on what is true, and honorable, and right, and pure, and lovely, and admirable. Think about things that are excellent and worthy of praise."

Philippians 4:8 (NLT)

If you live for weekends, holidays, and special occasions...you won't enjoy life.

If you keep others at arms length, are unwilling to compromise, insist on being right, resist love, reject correction, and refuse to apologize...you won't enjoy life.

If you're waiting on something to begin or end, a job or status to define you or relationship to complete you...you won't enjoy life.

If you allow others to determine your thoughts, mood, actions, worth, value or purpose...you won't enjoy life.

If you're stingy with your money or possessions, give others your leftovers, love conditionally, and withhold affection...you won't enjoy life.

If you hold onto blame, unforgiveness, envy, bitterness, compare yourself to others, are critical and negative, find it hard to laugh in general, or at yourself...you won't enjoy life.

If you're unwilling to be vulnerable, admit weaknesses, deny insecurities, have to have all the answers, hold onto regret and guilt, allow little room for error, find it difficult to ask for help, or hard to forgive yourself…you won't enjoy life.

But when you seek God first, release your hurts to Jesus, trust the prompting of the Holy Spirit, open up all of your heart to God's people and confess your unmet emotional needs, commit to understanding how negative behavior patterns steal God's promises, receive love, grace, and mercy, renew your mind with the Word daily, believe God supplies all your needs and that His strength is perfected in your weaknesses, pray about everything, cast your cares, believe the Word more than your feelings, walk by faith not sight, know that God purposed and planned you long ago, loves you more than all the stars in the sky, and that He will continue to do the good work He started in you until the day you see Jesus, *then you will know the truth and the truth will set you free…* and you will enjoy life!!!

Well friends, I wrote *Enjoying Life 101* years ago after reading several comments from "Christian" people who were posting their opinions and advice on social media. Some comments were ripping people apart, other were just "fake sounding", and then some were just complaining about everything. The childish part of me wanted to post: stop making Christians look mean, fake, and whiny.

Instead, I made a mature decision and put pen to paper and wrote out Enjoying Life 101 in a few minutes. My point is…*we have to be real if we want to heal*! This means intimately connecting with others, taking ownership of our life, opening our heart up to the grace we need to heal and transform, walking in the basics of love that Jesus modeled for us, and then...we will know the truth and the truth will set us free!!!

 I pray this handbook has helped you and that you will use it as a resource and reference guide. In the meantime, I would love to hear your thoughts, questions, and connect with you on social media. Below are the links so we can—take care! ♥LMM

* * * * *

Facebook	facebook.com/christianinsightforlife
Twitter	twitter.com/itslmm
Instagram	@itslmm
Pintrest	pintrest.com/christiancouns

Made in the USA
Columbia, SC
11 April 2022